JOURNEYS

Practice Book
Teacher's Edition

Grade 1

HOUGHTON MIFFLIN HARCOURT
School Publishers

ISBN-10:   0-547-27191-3
ISBN-13:   978-0-547-27191-0

2 3 4 5 6 7 8 9 10   0928   18 17 16 15 14 13 12 11 10
4500227466   A B C D E F G

Contents

Practice Book Volume 1

Practice Book Volume 2

Contents

Name _____

Listen for the Short *a* and *m* Sounds

Say each picture name. Listen for the short a sound. Write the letter a to show where you hear the short a sound.

1. a (1 point)
2. a (1)
3. a (1)

Say each picture name. Listen for the m sound. Write the letter m to show where you hear the sound for m.

4. m (1)
5. m (1)
6. m (1)

Name _____

Words to Know

Read the words in the box. Then read and finish the sentences.

Words to Know

am   I   to   like

I am   Responses will vary. (1 point)
_____

I like to   Responses will vary. (1)

Draw a picture to go with your sentences. (2)

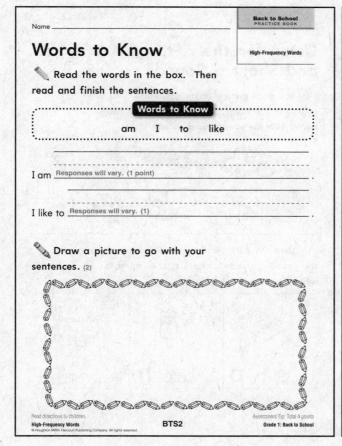

Name _____

Listen for the *s*, *m*, and Short *a* Sounds

Say each picture name. Listen for the /s/ sound. Write the letter s to show where you hear the sound for s.

1. s (1)
2. s (1)
3. s (1)

Listen to each picture name. Listen for the sounds. Use the letters s, a, or m to write the picture name. Remember that a person's name begins with a capital letter.

4. m (1) a (1) t
5. s (1) a (1) d
6. S (1) a (1) m (1)

Words to Know

Read the words in the box. Then read
the story.

Words to Know

a   see   the   I   to   like

I am Sam.

I see a 🐶.

I like the 🐶.

I see a 🐱.

I like the 🐱.

✏️ Draw what will happen next in the story. (2 points)

Read directions to children.
High-Frequency Words
© Houghton Mifflin Harcourt Publishing Company. All rights reserved.
Assessment Tip: Total 2 points.
BTS4
Grade 1: Back to School

Listen for the *t, s, m,* and Short *a* Sounds

✏️ Say each picture name. Listen for the *t*
sound. Write the letter *t* to show where you
hear the sound for *t*.

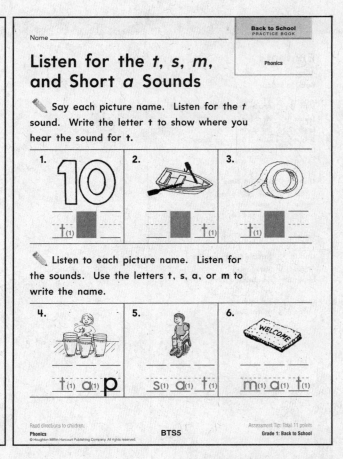

1.	2.	3.
t (1)	t (1)	t (1)

✏️ Listen to each picture name. Listen for
the sounds. Use the letters t, s, a, or m to
write the name.

4.	5.	6.
t (1) a (1) p	s (1) a (1) t (1)	m (1) a (1) t (1)

Read directions to children.
Phonics
© Houghton Mifflin Harcourt Publishing Company. All rights reserved.
Assessment Tip: Total 11 points
BTS5
Grade 1: Back to School

Words to Know

✏️ Read the words in the box. Then read
the story. Draw a line under the words that
have short a. (1 point each)

Words to Know

we   go   I   a   see   like   to   the

I am <u>Tam</u>.

I am <u>Sam</u>.

We see a <u>mat</u>.

We like the <u>mat</u>.

We go to the <u>mat</u>.

✏️ Draw what Sam and Tam will do next. (2)

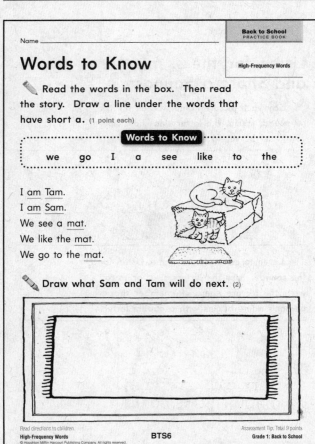

Read directions to children.
High-Frequency Words
© Houghton Mifflin Harcourt Publishing Company. All rights reserved.
Assessment Tip: Total 9 points
BTS6
Grade 1: Back to School

Listen for the *c, t, m,* and Short *a* Sounds

✏️ Say each picture name. Listen for the
sounds in the name. Color the pictures that
begin with the same sound as cat. (5 points)

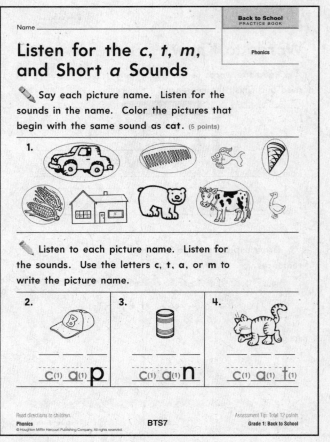

1.

✏️ Listen to each picture name. Listen for
the sounds. Use the letters c, t, a, or m to
write the picture name.

2.	3.	4.
c (1) a (1) p	c (1) a (1) n	c (1) a (1) t (1)

Read directions to children.
Phonics
© Houghton Mifflin Harcourt Publishing Company. All rights reserved.
Assessment Tip: Total 12 points
BTS7
Grade 1: Back to School

Words to Know

High-Frequency Words

✏️ Read the words in the box. Then read the story. Draw a line under the words that have short **a**. (1 point each)

Words to Know

> is are we go I a see like to the

We see Sam.
Sam is the cat.
Am I a cat?
Is Cam a cat?
We are the 🐭.
We like Sam.
We go to see Sam!

✏️ Draw what will happen next in the story. (2)

Letters and Sounds

Phonics

✏️ Trace and read the words. Draw a line from each word to its picture. (1 point each)

mat

cat

sat

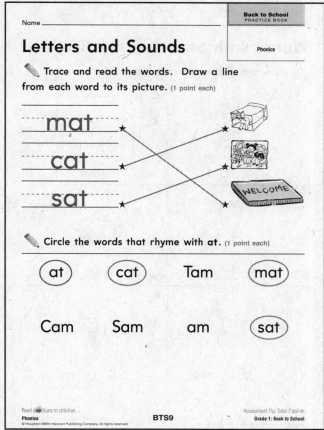

✏️ Circle the words that rhyme with **at**. (1 point each)

(at)   (cat)   Tam   (mat)

Cam   Sam   am   (sat)

Words to Know

High-Frequency Words

Read the words in the box. Then read the story.

Words to Know

> a are go I like is see the to we

We are at the 🏫.
We see a cat.
The cat is a 🐯.
I like the cat.
We like to go to the 🏫.

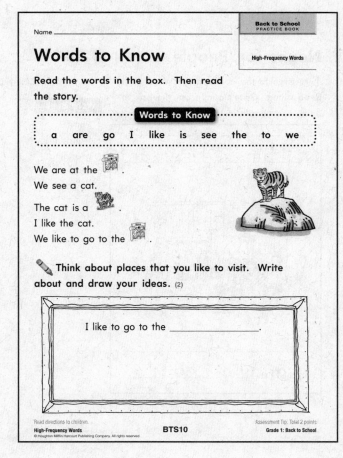

✏️ Think about places that you like to visit. Write about and draw your ideas. (2)

I like to go to the _____.

Words to Know

✏️ Complete the sentences. Write a word from the box on each line.

Words to Know

> with help and you play be

1. Look at Cam ___and___ Sam.   (1 point)

2. What will this ___be___ ?   (1)

3. I like to ___help___ .   (1)

4. She can ___play___ .   (1)

5. Come ___with___ me, Sam!   (1)

6. ___You___ can go down.   (1)

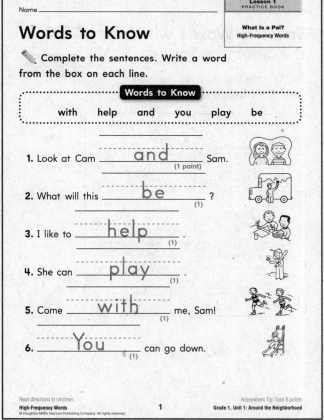

Name _____

Words with Short *a*

✏ Write the missing letter. Read the word.

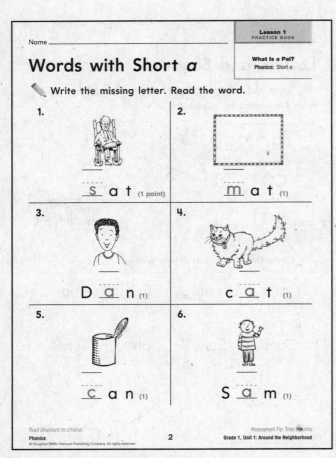

1. __s__ a t (1 point)

2. __m__ a t (1)

3. D __a__ n (1)

4. c __a__ t (1)

5. __c__ a n (1)

6. S __a__ m (1)

Name _____

Consonants *s, n, d*

✏ Name each picture. Think of the beginning sound. Write s, n, or d.

1. __s__ (1 point)

2. __n__ (1)

3. __d__ (1)

4. __n__ (1)

5. __s__ (1)

6. __d__ (1)

Name _____

Spelling Words with the Short *a* Sound

✏ Sort the words. Write the correct Spelling Words in each column.

Spelling Words

am
at
sat
man
dad
mat

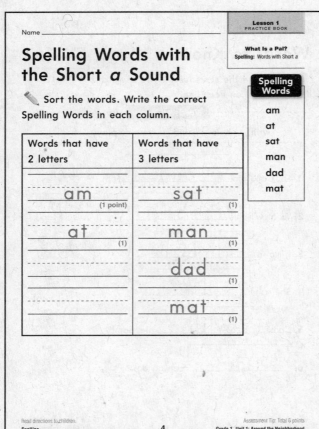

Words that have 2 letters	Words that have 3 letters
am (1 point)	sat (1)
at (1)	man (1)
	dad (1)
	mat (1)

Name _____

Nouns for People

✏ Listen to the nouns in the Word Bank. Read along. Write nouns from the box to name the people in the picture.

Word Bank

Pam
fireman
grandma
dad

Pam (2 points)   fireman (2)

grandma (2)   dad (2)

Giving Details

✏️ Listen to the words in the Word Bank. Read along. Add two details to this picture of two pals. Then write labels that tell who and what. Possible responses shown.

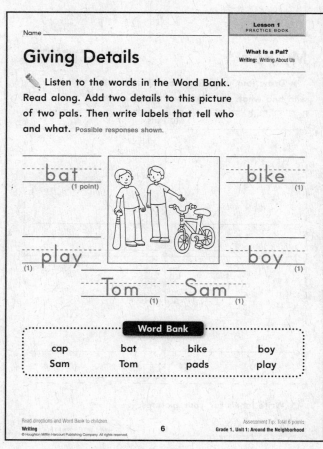

bat (1 point)

bike (1)

play (1)

boy (1)

Tom (1)   Sam (1)

Word Bank

cap	bat	bike	boy
Sam	Tom	pads	play

Consonants *p, f*

✏️ Name each picture. Think of the beginning sound. Write **p** or **f**.

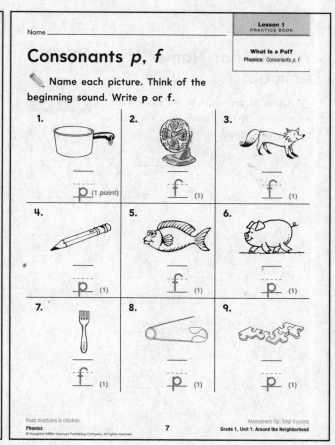

1. p (1 point)
2. f (1)
3. f (1)
4. p (1)
5. f (1)
6. p (1)
7. f (1)
8. p (1)
9. p (1)

Main Idea

✏️ The story is about pals. Write things from the story that tell about pals. Possible responses shown.

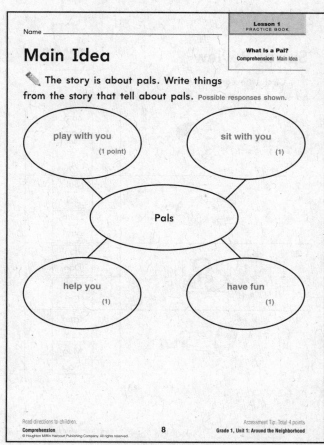

play with you (1 point)

sit with you (1)

Pals

help you (1)

have fun (1)

Spelling Words with the Short *a* Sound

✏️ Write the missing letter to complete each Spelling Word. Then write the word.

Spelling Words

am
at
sat
man
dad
mat

1. s a t   sat (1 point)

2. m a n   man (1)

3. m a t   mat (1)

4. a t   at (1)

5. d a d   dad (1)

6. a m   am (1)

Panel 1 (top-left)

Words That Name Animals

✏️ Listen to the nouns in the Word Bank. Read along. Write a noun from the box to name each picture.

Word Bank
- mouse
- bird
- dog
- cat
- bear

1. bird
(2 points)

2. bear
(2)

3. mouse
(2)

4. cat
(2)

5. dog
(2)

Panel 2 (top-right)

My Pals

✏️ Draw four pals. Show details that tell who and what. Responses will vary. (1 point each)

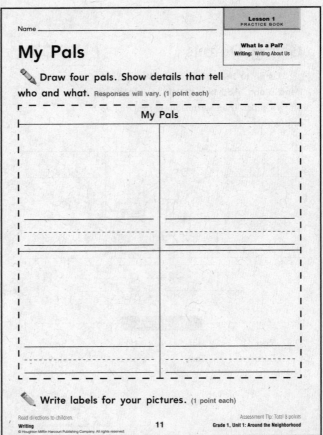

My Pals

✏️ Write labels for your pictures. (1 point each)

Panel 3 (bottom-left)

Spelling Words with the Short a Sound

✏️ Write the correct word to complete each sentence.

1. This **mat** is for the cat. (mat, dad)
(1 point)

2. I **sat** with it. (dad, sat)
(1)

3. I **am** mad. (mat, am)
(1)

4. Pat is **at** the play. (at, am)
(1)

5. We like the **man**. (man, at)
(1)

6. We sat on **dad**. (at, dad)
(1)

Panel 4 (bottom-right)

Spiral Review

✏️ Circle the correct word in each box to name each person and pet.

1. (2 points)
sam / **Sam**
al / **Al**

2. (2)
Sal / sal
Gam / gam

3. (2)
dan / **Dan**
cal / **Cal**

4. (2)
Cam / cam
Mag / mag

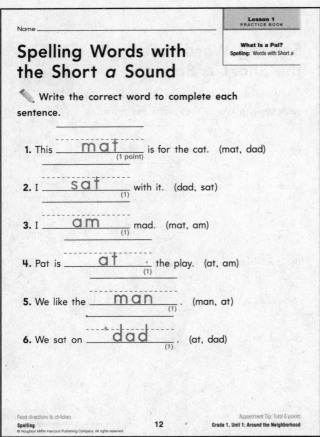

Grammar in Writing

Words that name people and animals are called **nouns**. Use nouns to name people and animals when you write.

The <u>boy</u> smiles.
The <u>dog</u> runs.

Listen to the nouns in the Word Bank, and to the sentences. Read along. Look at the picture. Write nouns from the box to finish the sentences.

Word Bank
dad
girl
cat
boy

1. The ___girl___ plays.
   (2 points)

2. The ___dad___ cooks.
   (2)

3. The ___boy___ helps.
   (2)

4. The ___cat___ sleeps.
   (2)

Words to Know

Complete the sentences. Write a word from the box on each line.

Words to Know
he   look   have   too   for   what

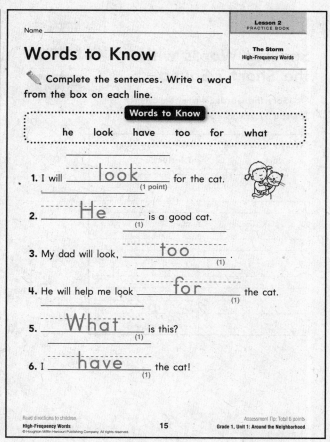

1. I will ___look___ for the cat.
   (1 point)

2. ___He___ is a good cat.
   (1)

3. My dad will look, ___too___ .
   (1)

4. He will help me look ___for___ the cat.
   (1)

5. ___What___ is this?
   (1)

6. I ___have___ the cat!
   (1)

Words with Short *i*

Write the missing letter. Read the word.

1. s_i_t (1 point)

2. T_i_m (1)

3. p_i_n (1)

4. f_i_n (1)

5. s_i_p (1)

6. h_i_t (1)

Consonants *r, h, /z/s*

Write the missing letter. Read the word.

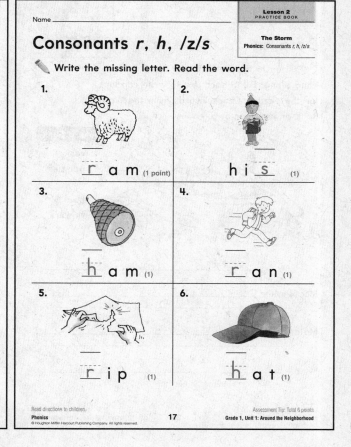

1. _r_ a m (1 point)

2. h i _s_ (1)

3. _h_ a m (1)

4. _r_ a n (1)

5. _r_ i p (1)

6. _h_ a t (1)

Spelling Words with the Short *i* Sound

✏️ Sort the words. Write the correct Spelling Words in each column.

Spelling Words

if
is
him
rip
fit
pin

Words that have 2 letters	Words that have 3 letters
if (1 point)	him (1)
is (1)	rip (1)
	fit (1)
	pin (1)

Nouns for Places

✏️ Listen to the nouns in the Word Bank. Read along. Write nouns from the box to name the places in the pictures.

Word Bank

pool   city   beach   park

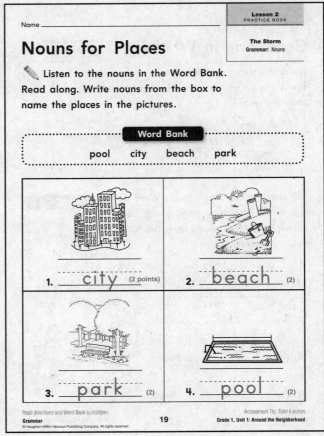

1. city (2 points)   2. beach (2)

3. park (2)   4. pool (2)

Details

✏️ Listen to the words in the Word Bank. Read along. Fill in each line to write captions for the picture. Choose words from the Word Bank or use your own. **Responses will vary.**

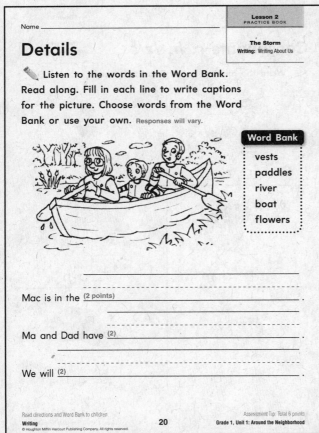

Word Bank

vests
paddles
river
boat
flowers

Mac is in the (2 points) _____

Ma and Dad have (2) _____

We will (2) _____

Consonants *b*, *g*

✏️ Name each picture. Think of the ending sound. Write **b** or **g**.

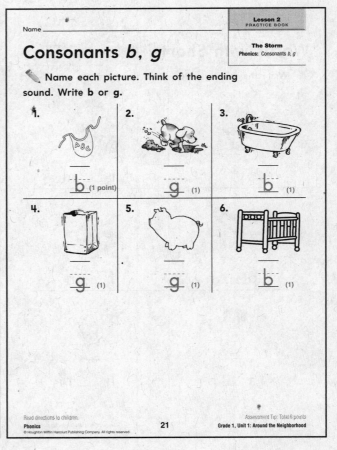

1. b (1 point)   2. g (1)   3. b (1)

4. g (1)   5. g (1)   6. b (1)

Understanding Characters

✏️ Write or draw things Pop said in the story in the **Speaking** box. Write or draw things Pop did in the **Acting** box.

Speaking	Acting
Tim has fun with Pop. Pop tells Tim to go to bed. (2 points)	Pop plays with Tim. Pop looks at the clock. Pop gives Tim some milk. Pop gives Tim a hug. (4)

Spelling Words with the Short *i* Sound

✏️ Write the missing letter to complete each Spelling Word. Then write the word.

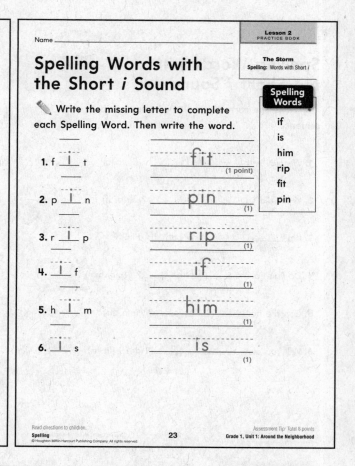

Spelling Words

if
is
him
rip
fit
pin

1. f _i_ t   fit (1 point)

2. p _i_ n   pin (1)

3. r _i_ p   rip (1)

4. _i_ f   if (1)

5. h _i_ m   him (1)

6. _i_ s   is (1)

Words That Name Things

✏️ Listen to the nouns in the Word Bank. Read along. Write a noun from the box to name each thing.

Word Bank

lamp
milk
door
chair
book

1. book (2 points)

2. milk (2)

3. chair (2)

4. door (2)

5. lamp (2)

Planning My Caption

✏️ Draw a picture of your family in a favorite place.

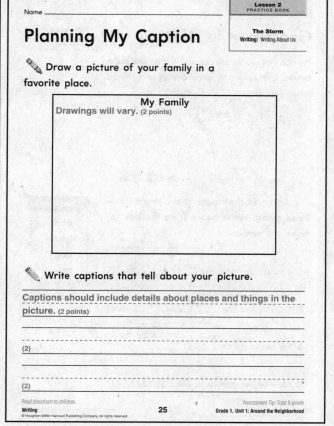

My Family
Drawings will vary. (2 points)

✏️ Write captions that tell about your picture.

Captions should include details about places and things in the picture. (2 points)

(2)

(2)

Spelling Words with the Short *i* Sound

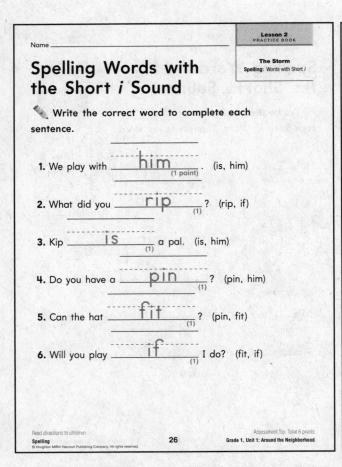 Write the correct word to complete each sentence.

1. We play with ___him___ . (is, him)
(1 point)

2. What did you ___rip___ ? (rip, if)
(1)

3. Kip ___is___ a pal. (is, him)
(1)

4. Do you have a ___pin___ ? (pin, him)
(1)

5. Can the hat ___fit___ ? (pin, fit)
(1)

6. Will you play ___if___ I do? (fit, if)
(1)

Spiral Review

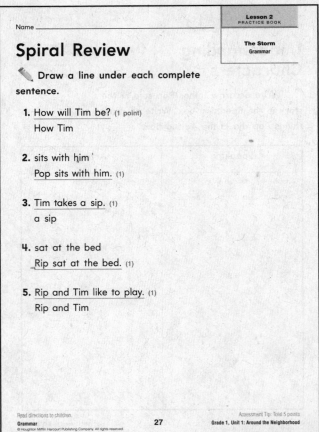 Draw a line under each complete sentence.

1. How will Tim be? (1 point)
How Tim

2. sits with him
Pop sits with him. (1)

3. Tim takes a sip. (1)
a sip

4. sat at the bed
Rip sat at the bed. (1)

5. Rip and Tim like to play. (1)
Rip and Tim

Grammar in Writing

Words that name places and things are called **nouns**. Use nouns to name places and things when you write.

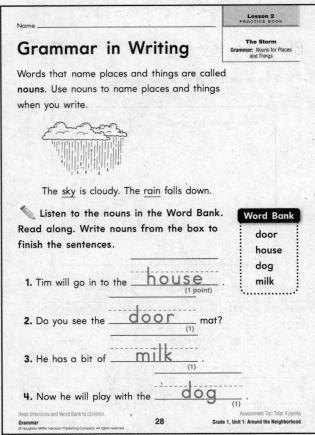

The sky is cloudy. The rain falls down.

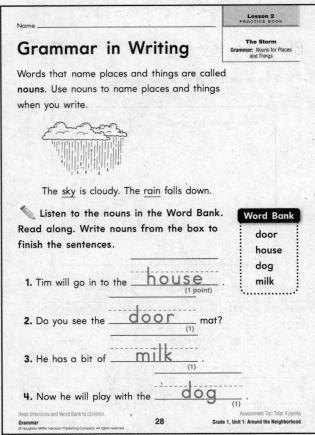 Listen to the nouns in the Word Bank. Read along. Write nouns from the box to finish the sentences.

Word Bank
door
house
dog
milk

1. Tim will go in to the ___house___
(1 point)

2. Do you see the ___door___ mat?
(1)

3. He has a bit of ___milk___ .
(1)

4. Now he will play with the ___dog___ .
(1)

Words to Know

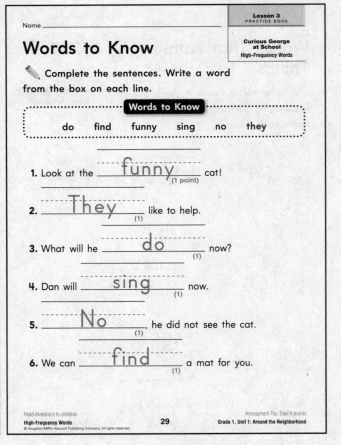 Complete the sentences. Write a word from the box on each line.

Words to Know
do   find   funny   sing   no   they

1. Look at the ___funny___ cat!
(1 point)

2. ___They___ like to help.
(1)

3. What will he ___do___ now?
(1)

4. Dan will ___sing___ now.
(1)

5. ___No___ , he did not see the cat.
(1)

6. We can ___find___ a mat for you.
(1)

Name _____

Words with Short o

✏️ Name each picture. Color the pictures
with short o.

(1) cot

(1) dog

(1) mop

(1) top

(1) pot

Name _____

Lesson 3
PRACTICE BOOK

Curious George
at School
Phonics: Consonants l, x

Consonants l, x

✏️ Finish the rhymes. Write one of the
words from the box on the line.

six   box

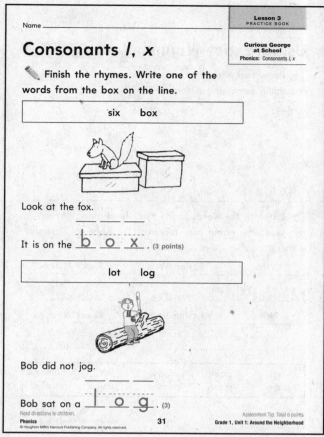

Look at the fox.

It is on the b o x . (3 points)

lot   log

Bob did not jog.

Bob sat on a l o g . (3)

Name _____

Lesson 3
PRACTICE BOOK

Curious George at
School
Spelling: Words with Short o

Spelling Words with
the Short o Sound

✏️ Sort the words. Write the correct
Spelling Words in each column.

**Spelling
Words**

log
dot
top
hot
lot
ox

Words that rhyme	Words that do not rhyme
dot (1 point)	log (1)
hot (1)	top (1)
lot (1)	ox (1)

Name _____

Lesson 3
PRACTICE BOOK

Curious George
at School
Grammar: Action Verbs

Action Verbs

✏️ Listen to the verbs in the Word Bank.
Read along. Write verbs from the box to tell
about the actions in the pictures.

Word Bank

eat
run
drink
draw

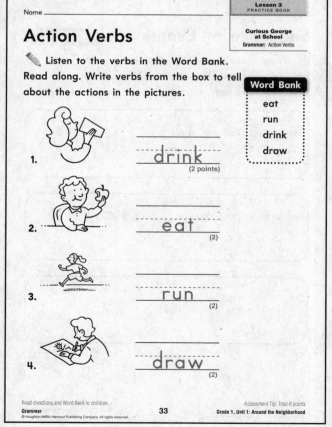

1. drink
(2 points)

2. eat
(2)

3. run
(2)

4. draw
(2)

Using Exact Nouns

✏️ Draw two people at school. Show each one doing something different.

```
┌ ─ ─ ─ ─ ─ ─ ─ ─ ─ ─ ┬ ─ ─ ─ ─ ─ ─ ─ ─ ─ ─ ┐
(1 point)              (1)
│                      │                      │


│                      │                      │


└ ─ ─ ─ ─ ─ ─ ─ ─ ─ ─ ┴ ─ ─ ─ ─ ─ ─ ─ ─ ─ ─ ┘
```

✏️ Listen to the words in the box. Read along. Write two sentences about your pictures. Tell what each person is doing. Possible responses shown.

Who	Action Verb	Exact Noun
My teacher (1)	reads (1)	a book. (1)

Who	Action Verb	Exact Noun
I (1)	cut (1)	paper. (1)

ball	book	drum	fish	games
paper	piano	picture	song	teacher

Words with Inflection -s

✏️ Name each picture. Write the word. Use words in the box.

sits	digs	pats	sips	bats	mops

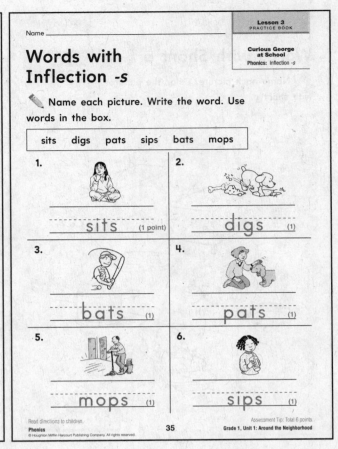

1. sits (1 point)
2. digs (1)
3. bats (1)
4. pats (1)
5. mops (1)
6. sips (1)

Sequence of Events

✏️ Write in the chart the events that happen in the story. Tell what happens first, next, and last.

First
George meets the class. (2 points)

↓

Next
George makes a big mess. (2)

↓

Last
The children help George. (2)

Spelling Words with the Short o Sound

Spelling Words
log
dot
hot
top
lot
ox

✏️ Write the missing letter to complete each Spelling Word. Then write the word.

1. l O t   lot (1 point)
2. l O g   log (1)
3. h O t   hot (1)
4. O x   ox (1)
5. t O p   top (1)
6. d O t   dot (1)

More Words That Show Action

✎ Listen to the verbs in the Word Bank. Read along. Write a verb from the box to name each action in the picture.

Word Bank

climb
slide
jump
swing
throw

slide
(2 points)

climb
(2)

swing
(2)

throw
(2)

jump
(2)

Planning My Sentences

✎ Write an action verb at the top of each box. Draw a picture to go with the verb.

Possible responses shown.

(1 point) read
(1)

(1) paint
(1)

Spelling Words with the Short *o* Sound

✎ Write the correct word to complete each sentence.

1. A _____dot_____ is not big. (hot, dot)
   (1 point)

2. The _____log_____ is big. (log, hot)
   (1)

3. We have a _____lot_____ of cats. (lot, top)
   (1)

4. Pam is at the _____top_____. (dog, top)
   (1)

5. Do you have a _____hot_____ pot? (hot, log)
   (1)

6. Did you ever see an _____ox_____? (ox, hot)
   (1)

Spiral Review

✎ Draw a line under each correct statement.

1. We get the box. (1 point)
   we get the box.

2. Bob can help
   Bob can help. (1)

3. He will mix it. (1)
   he will mix it.

4. We have fun. (1)
   we have fun

5. We like to sing
   We like to sing. (1)

Name _____

Lesson 3
PRACTICE BOOK

Curious George
at School
Grammar: Action Verbs

Grammar in Writing

Words that tell what people and animals
do are called **verbs**.

> They <u>run</u> on the playground.

🖊 Circle the verb to finish each sentence.
Write the verb on the line.

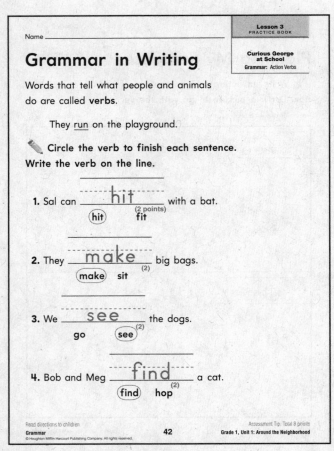

1. Sal can ___hit___ with a bat.
(2 points)
(hit) fit

2. They ___make___ big bags.
(make) sit (2)

3. We ___see___ the dogs.
go (see) (2)

4. Bob and Meg ___find___ a cat.
(find) hop (2)

Words to Know

🖊 Complete the sentences. Write a word
from the box on each line.

Words to Know

| all | does | here | me | my | who |

1. Lin is ___my___ pal.
(1 point)

2. Sam will come ___here___ to play.
(1)

3. He likes to play with ___me___ .
(1)

4. I will see ___who___ is there.
(1)

5. Sam ___does___ a funny trick.
(1)

6. We will take up ___all___ the mats.
(1)

Words with Short *e*

🖊 Circle the word that matches
each picture.

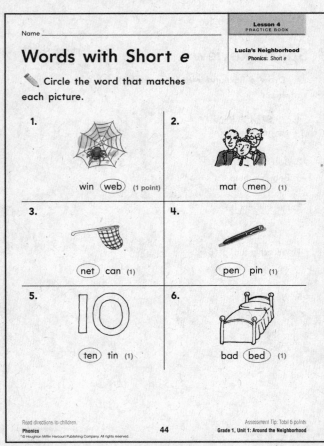

1. win (web) (1 point)

2. mat (men) (1)

3. (net) can (1)

4. (pen) pin (1)

5. (ten) tin (1)

6. bad (bed) (1)

Consonants *y, w*

🖊 Name each picture. Think of the
beginning sound. Write y or w.

1. ___y___ (1 point)

2. ___w___ (1)

3. ___y___ (1)

4. ___w___ (1)

5. ___w___ (1)

6. ___y___ (1)

Spelling Words with the Short *e* Sound

Lesson 4
PRACTICE BOOK

Lucia's Neighborhood
Spelling: Words with Short *e*

✎ Sort the words. Write the correct Spelling Words in each column.

Spelling Words

yet
web
pen
wet
leg
hen

Words that rhyme with **get**	Words that rhyme with **den**	Words that do not rhyme
yet (1 point)	pen (1)	web (1)
wet (1)	hen (1)	leg (1)

Adjectives for Size

Lesson 4
PRACTICE BOOK

Lucia's Neighborhood
Grammar: Adjectives for Size and Shape

✎ Listen to the adjectives. Read along. Circle the adjective that describes what the picture shows. Write the adjective.

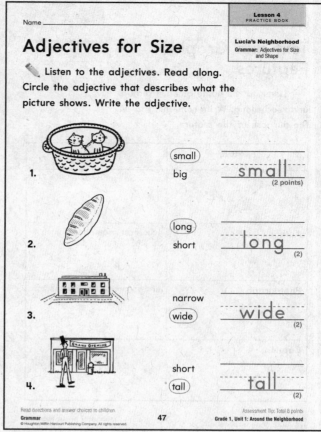

1. (small) big   small (2 points)

2. (long) short   long (2)

3. narrow (wide)   wide (2)

4. short (tall)   tall (2)

Using Words That Are Just Right

Lesson 4
PRACTICE BOOK

Lucia's Neighborhood
Writing: Writing About Us

✎ Cross out the word that is the same in each sentence. Listen to the words in the box. Read along. Write a better word from the box.

Word Bank

busy	large	new	sweet
round	kind	square	tall

Possible responses shown:

1. Our town has a good market.   busy (2 points)

2. Mom and I get good apples there.   sweet (2)

3. We got a good cake for Dad.   round (2)

4. The man that helps us is good.   kind (2)

Consonants *k, v, j*

Lesson 4
PRACTICE BOOK

Lucia's Neighborhood
Phonics: Consonants *k, v, j*

✎ Name each picture. Think of the beginning sound. Write k, v, or j.

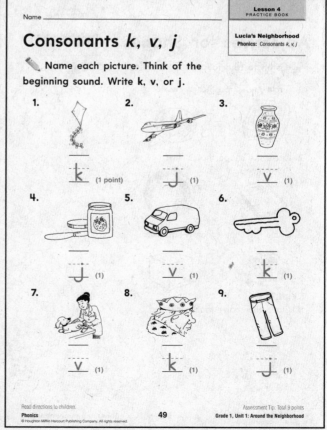

1. k (1 point)   2. j (1)   3. v (1)

4. j (1)   5. v (1)   6. k (1)

7. v (1)   8. k (1)   9. j (1)

Name _____

Lesson 4
PRACTICE BOOK

Lucia's Neighborhood
Comprehension: Text and
Graphic Features

Text and Graphic Features

✏️ Listen to the name of each feature and read along. Write something to tell the purpose of the feature.

Feature	Purpose
Title	tells name of book (1 point)
Author	tells who wrote the book (1)
Photograph	shows people and places (1)
Caption	names things in pictures (1)

Spelling Words with the Short *e* Sound

✏️ Write the missing letter to complete each Spelling Word. Then write the word.

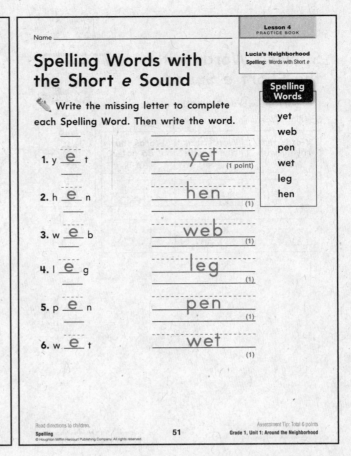

Spelling Words

yet
web
pen
wet
leg
hen

1. y _e_ t _____ yet (1 point)

2. h _e_ n _____ hen (1)

3. w _e_ b _____ web (1)

4. l _e_ g _____ leg (1)

5. p _e_ n _____ pen (1)

6. w _e_ t _____ wet (1)

Adjectives for Shape

✏️ Listen to and follow the directions.

1. Circle the shape that is **round**.

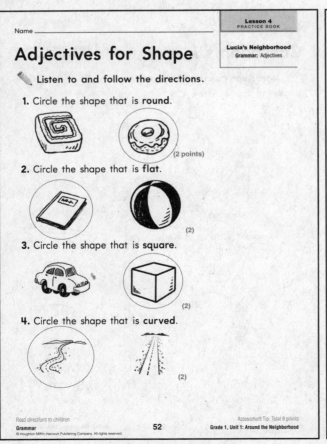

(2 points)

2. Circle the shape that is **flat**.

(2)

3. Circle the shape that is **square**.

(2)

4. Circle the shape that is **curved**.

(2)

Spelling Words with the Short *e* Sound

✏️ Write the correct word to complete each sentence.

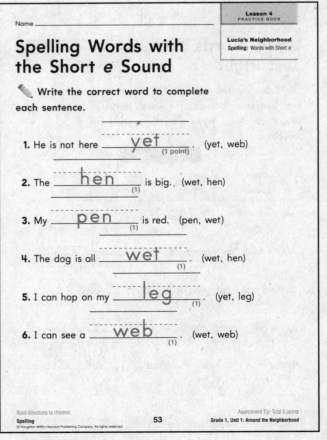

1. He is not here ___ yet ___ . (yet, web) (1 point)

2. The ___ hen ___ is big. (wet, hen) (1)

3. My ___ pen ___ is red. (pen, wet) (1)

4. The dog is all ___ wet ___ . (wet, hen) (1)

5. I can hop on my ___ leg ___ . (yet, leg) (1)

6. I can see a ___ web ___ . (wet, web) (1)

Name _____

Spiral Review

✏️ Circle the end mark in each sentence.
Then circle **statement** or **question**.

1. What can you find(?)

statement
(question) (2)

2. I can find a fan(.)

(statement)
question (2)

3. What will you do now(?)

statement
(question) (2)

4. I will sing(.)

(statement)
question (2)

5. Do you have a pet(?)

statement
(question) (2)

6. Yes, I have a pet dog(.)

(statement)
question (2)

Name _____

Lesson 4
PRACTICE BOOK

Lucia's Neighborhood
Grammar: Adjectives for Size
and Shape

Grammar in Writing

Words that describe people, animals, or things
are called **adjectives**. Adjectives can describe
size or shape.

The house is <u>big</u>. (size)
The truck is <u>wide</u>. (shape)

✏️ Listen to the adjectives in the Word
Banks. Read along. Write on the line an
adjective for size.

Word Bank
long
little

1. A leg is ___long___ .
(1 point)

2. A dot is ___little___ .
(1)

✏️ Write on the line an adjective for shape.

Word Bank
flat
round

3. A map is ___flat___ .
(1)

4. A log is ___round___ .
(1)

Words to Know

✏️ Draw a line to the word that completes
the sentence. Write the word on the line.

1. Tom will ___pull___ the sled.
(1 point)

hold

2. It was ___good___ to sit for a bit.
(1)

full

3. All the bags are ___full___ .
(1)

pull

4. Mel has ___many___ pals.
(1)

friend

5. Cam is my ___friend___ .
(1)

good

6. Mom will ___hold___ my books for me.
(1)

many

Words with Short *u*

✏️ Write the missing letter. Read the word.

1.
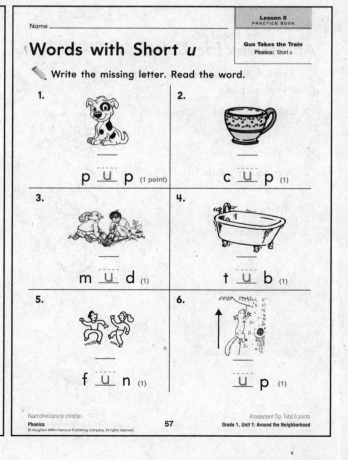
p _u_ p (1 point)

2.
c _u_ p (1)

3.
m _u_ d (1)

4.
t _u_ b (1)

5.
f _u_ n (1)

6.
_u_ p (1)

More Words With Short *u*

✏️ Write the missing letter. Read the word.

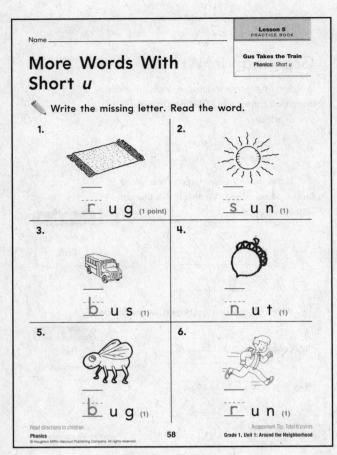

1.
r u g (1 point)

2.
s u n (1)

3.
b u s (1)

4.
n u t (1)

5.
b u g (1)

6.
r u n (1)

Spelling Words with the Short *u* Sound

✏️ Sort the words. Write the correct Spelling Words in each column.

Spelling Words

up
bug
mud
nut
hug
tub

Words that rhyme	Words that do not rhyme
bug (1 point)	up (1)
hug (1)	mud (1)
	nut (1)
	tub (1)

Adjectives for Color

✏️ Listen to the directions. Read along. Color each picture.

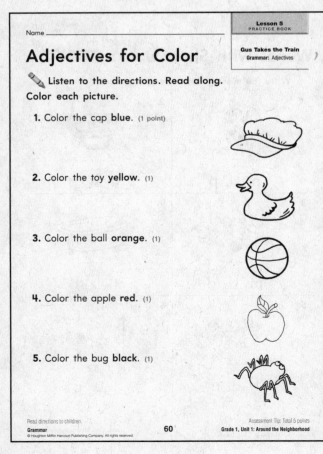

1. Color the cap **blue**. (1 point)

2. Color the toy **yellow**. (1)

3. Color the ball **orange**. (1)

4. Color the apple **red**. (1)

5. Color the bug **black**. (1)

Telling More

✏️ Complete each sentence. Choose an adjective from the box to tell more. Possible responses shown:

big	many	ten	mad
bad	good	red	tan
sad	funny	hot	wet

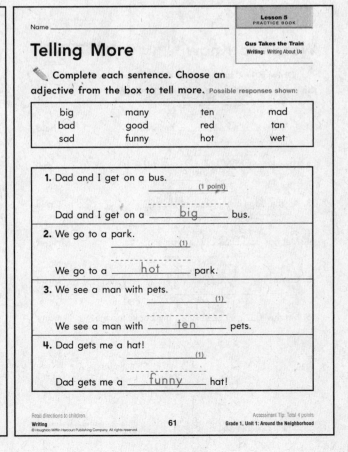

1. Dad and I get on a bus. (1 point)

Dad and I get on a ___big___ bus.

2. We go to a park. (1)

We go to a ___hot___ park.

3. We see a man with pets. (1)

We see a man with ___ten___ pets.

4. Dad gets me a hat! (1)

Dad gets me a ___funny___ hat!

Consonants *qu*, *z*

✏️ Name each picture. Think of the
beginning sound. Write **qu** or **z**.

1. __qu__ (1 point)

2. __z__ (1)

3. __qu__ (1)

4. __z__ (1)

5. __z__ (1)

6. __qu__ (1)

Story Structure

✏️ Write or draw pictures to show the
characters, setting, and plot of the story.

Characters Gus, the conductor, and Peg (1 point)	Setting train station (1)
Plot	
Beginning Gus catches the train. (1)	
Middle Gus rides on the train. (1)	
End The train stops at the zoo. (1)	

Spelling Words with the Short *u* Sound

✏️ Write the missing letter to complete
each Spelling Word. Then write the word.

Spelling Words

up
bug
mud
nut
hug
tub

1. n __u__ t   __nut__ (1 point)

2. b __u__ g   __bug__ (1)

3. m __u__ d   __mud__ (1)

4. __u__ p   __up__ (1)

5. t __u__ b   __tub__ (1)

6. h __u__ g   __hug__ (1)

Adjectives for Number

✏️ Listen to the adjectives in the Word
Bank. Read along. Write a word from the
box to describe each picture.

Word Bank

two   three   four   six

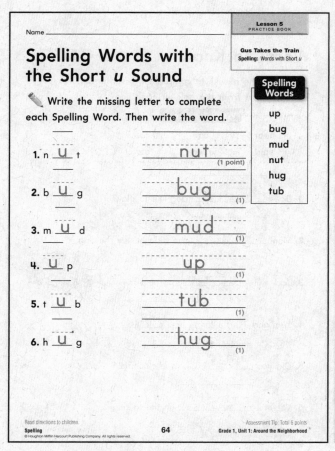

1. __six__ (1 point)

2. __two__ (1)

3. __three__ (1)

4. __four__ (1)

Spelling Words with the Short *u* Sound

Name _____

✏️ Write the correct word to complete each sentence.

1. Dad likes to _____ **hug** _____ the cat.   (up, hug)
   (1 point)

2. A _____ **bug** _____ is on my leg!   (bug, hug)
   (1)

3. Put the mat _____ **up** _____ on top.   (nut, up)
   (1)

4. I got wet in the _____ **tub** _____.   (tub, bug)
   (1)

5. Do you have a _____ **nut** _____ for me?   (nut, mud)
   (1)

6. The pig likes to play in the _____ **mud** _____.
   (mud, hug)   (1)

Spiral Review

Name _____

✏️ Circle the pronoun that can take the place of the underlined word or words. Then write the pronoun.

1. The box is full.

   _____ **It** _____ is full.
   (2 points)
   (It)   They

2. Peg and Ned play.

   _____ **They** _____ play.
   (2)
   She   (They)

3. Ted helps.

   _____ **He** _____ helps.
   (2)
   (He)   It

4. Nan has fun.

   _____ **She** _____ has fun.
   (2)
   They   (She)

Grammar in Writing

Name _____

Words that describe people, places, animals, or things are called **adjectives**. Adjectives can describe color and number.

The train is black. The five seats are red.

✏️ Finish each sentence with an adjective for number. Use the Word Bank.

Word Bank
one
three

1. I see _____ **three** _____ flowers.
   (2 points)

2. I see _____ **one** _____ cat.
   (2)

✏️ Listen to and follow the directions.

3. Draw **two** apples.
   Color the apples **red.** (2)

4. Draw **four** bugs.
   Color the bugs **black.** (2)

Words to Know

Name _____

✏️ Fill in the blanks to complete the sentences. Write a word from the box on each line.

Words to Know

| hear | call | come |
| said | every | away |

1. Does _____ **every** _____ dog like to play?
   (1 point)

2. Mem _____ **said** _____ she did not see the dog.
   (1)

3. Jack will _____ **come** _____ to help me.
   (1)

4. Sam and Jill are far _____ **away** _____.
   (1)

5. Did you _____ **hear** _____ the clock tick?
   (1)

6. Von will _____ **call** _____ on me to sing.
   (1)

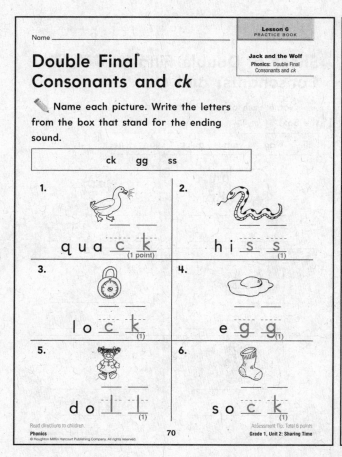

Name _____

Lesson 6
PRACTICE BOOK

Jack and the Wolf
Phonics: Double Final
Consonants and *ck*

Double Final Consonants and *ck*

✏ Name each picture. Write the letters from the box that stand for the ending sound.

ck	gg	ss

1. qua c k (1 point)

2. hi s s (1)

3. lo c k (1)

4. e g g (1)

5. do l l (1)

6. so c k (1)

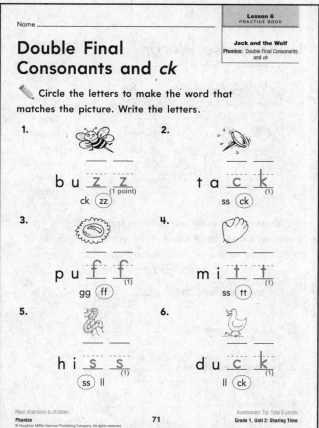

Name _____

Lesson 6
PRACTICE BOOK

Jack and the Wolf
Phonics: Double Final Consonants
and *ck*

Double Final Consonants and *ck*

✏ Circle the letters to make the word that matches the picture. Write the letters.

1. bu z z (1 point)   ck (zz)

2. ta c k (1)   ss (ck)

3. pu f f (1)   gg (ff)

4. mi t t (1)   ss (tt)

5. hi s s (1)   (ss) ll

6. du c k (1)   ll (ck)

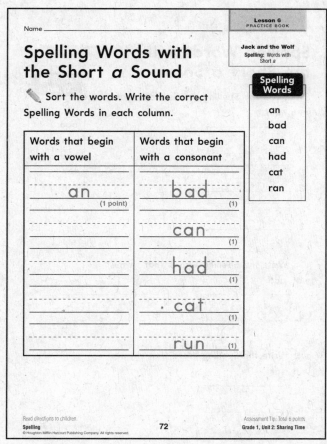

Name _____

Lesson 6
PRACTICE BOOK

Jack and the Wolf
Spelling: Words with
Short *a*

Spelling Words with the Short *a* Sound

✏ Sort the words. Write the correct Spelling Words in each column.

Spelling Words

an
bad
can
had
cat
ran

Words that begin with a vowel	Words that begin with a consonant
an (1 point)	bad (1)
	can (1)
	had (1)
	cat (1)
	run (1)

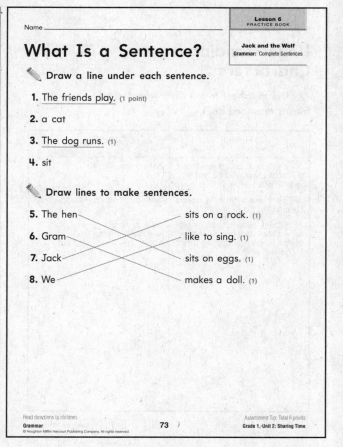

What Is a Sentence?

✏ Draw a line under each sentence.

1. The friends play. (1 point)

2. a cat

3. The dog runs. (1)

4. sit

✏ Draw lines to make sentences.

5. The hen — sits on a rock. (1)

6. Gram — like to sing. (1)

7. Jack — sits on eggs. (1)

8. We — makes a doll. (1)

Using Sense Words

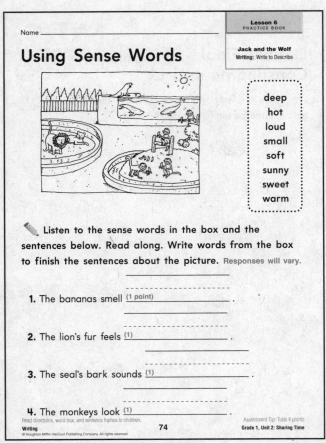

✏️ Listen to the sense words in the box and the sentences below. Read along. Write words from the box to finish the sentences about the picture. Responses will vary.

| deep |
| hot |
| loud |
| small |
| soft |
| sunny |
| sweet |
| warm |

1. The bananas smell (1 point) _____ .

2. The lion's fur feels (1) _____

3. The seal's bark sounds (1) _____ .

4. The monkeys look (1) _____

Read directions, word box, and sentence frames to children.

Writing
© Houghton Mifflin Harcourt Publishing Company. All rights reserved.

74

Assessment Tip: Total 4 points
Grade 1, Unit 2: Sharing Time

Short *a*, Double Final Consonants, and *ck*

✏️ Name each picture. Write words from the box.

| fill | wag | yam | quick | van | neck |

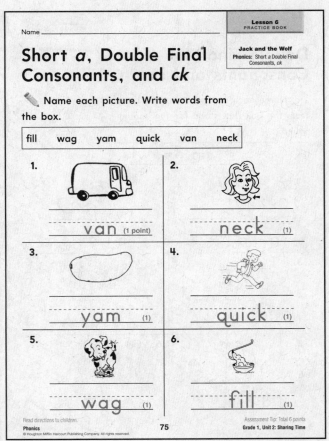

1. __van__ (1 point)

2. __neck__ (1)

3. __yam__ (1)

4. __quick__ (1)

5. __wag__ (1)

6. __fill__ (1)

Read directions to children.

Phonics
© Houghton Mifflin Harcourt Publishing Company. All rights reserved.

75

Assessment Tip: Total 6 points
Grade 1, Unit 2: Sharing Time

Understanding Characters

✏️ Use the chart to tell what Jack and his friends think and do.

Thinking	Acting
Jack thinks it is not fun to sit. He thinks it would be fun to yell "Wolf!" (1 point)	Jack yells, "Wolf!" (1)
Jack's friends think he needs help. (1)	Jack's friends run up the hill. Jack laughs. (1)
Jack thinks his friends don't care about him because they didn't come the second time he called wolf. (1)	Jack promises to be good and not trick his friends again. (1)

Read directions to children.

Comprehension
© Houghton Mifflin Harcourt Publishing Company. All rights reserved.

76

Assessment Tip: Total 6 points
Grade 1, Unit 2: Sharing Time

Spelling Words with the Short *a* Sound

✏️ Write the Spelling Words that rhyme with **man**.

1. __an__ (1 point)

2. __can__ (1)

3. __ran__ (1)

Spelling Words

an
bad
can
had
cat
ran

✏️ Write the Spelling Words that rhyme with **dad**.

4. __bad__ (1)

5. __had__ (1)

✏️ Write the Spelling Word that rhymes with **sat**.

6. __cat__ (1)

Read directions to children.

Spelling
© Houghton Mifflin Harcourt Publishing Company. All rights reserved.

77

Assessment Tip: Total 6 points
Grade 1, Unit 2: Sharing Time

Name _____

Is It a Sentence?

✏️ Draw a line under each sentence.

1. The dog naps. (1 point)
naps

2. Tim and Jim
Tim and Jim run away. (1)

3. the friends
The friends come to help. (1)

4. The man sits down. (1)
sits

5. sings
He sings. (1)

6. get up
The dog will get up. (1)

Name _____

Planning My Sentences

✏️ Listen to the labels in the web and read along. Write and draw details that describe your topic. You do not have to write words for every sense. Responses will vary.

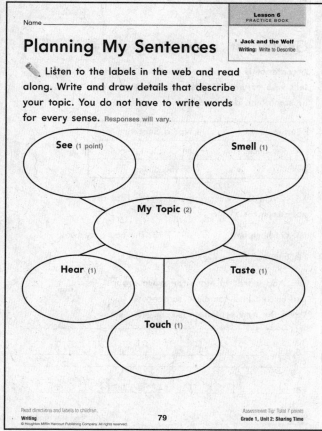

See (1 point)

Smell (1)

My Topic (2)

Hear (1)

Taste (1)

Touch (1)

Name _____

Spelling Words with the Short *a* Sound

✏️ Write a Spelling Word from the box to complete each sentence.

Spelling Words
bad
can
cat

1. Does this hat look ___bad___ ?
(1 point)

2. The ___cat___ will play with Jack.
(1)

3. ___Can___ you help me?
(1)

✏️ Write a Spelling Word from the box to complete each sentence.

Spelling Words
an
had
ran

4. I ___had___ to find my mitt.
(1)

5. She will make ___an___ egg for Meg.
(1)

6. I ___ran___ out to play.
(1)

Name _____

Spiral Review

✏️ Listen to the nouns in the Word Bank. Read along. Write a noun from the box to name each picture.

Word Bank
girl
pig
horse
baby

1. ___pig___
(1 point)

2. ___girl___
(1)

3. ___horse___
(1)

4. ___baby___
(1)

Lesson 6
PRACTICE BOOK

Jack and the Wolf
Grammar: Complete Sentences

Grammar in Writing

A **sentence** is a group of words. A sentence tells who or what. It also tells what someone or something does or did.

Sentence	Not a Sentence
All the ducks sit.	sit
	all the ducks

✏️ Circle the two groups of words that are not sentences.

1. We have fun.   **3.** The dog runs away.

2. (get mad) (1 point)   **4.** (Jack) (1)

✏️ Add words to make the word groups you circled into complete sentences.
Write the new sentences. Possible responses shown.

5. People get mad. (2 points)

6. Jack plays a trick. (2)

Lesson 7
PRACTICE BOOK

How Animals Communicate
High-Frequency Words

Words to Know

✏️ Fill in the blanks to complete the sentences.

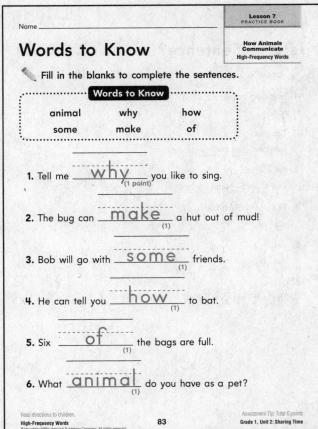

Words to Know

animal	why	how
some	make	of

1. Tell me __why__ (1 point) you like to sing.

2. The bug can __make__ (1) a hut out of mud!

3. Bob will go with __some__ (1) friends.

4. He can tell you __how__ (1) to bat.

5. Six __of__ (1) the bags are full.

6. What __animal__ (1) do you have as a pet?

Lesson 7
PRACTICE BOOK

How Animals Communicate
Phonics: Clusters with r

Clusters with *r*

✏️ Name each picture. Write letters from the box to complete the word.

br	cr	dr	gr	tr

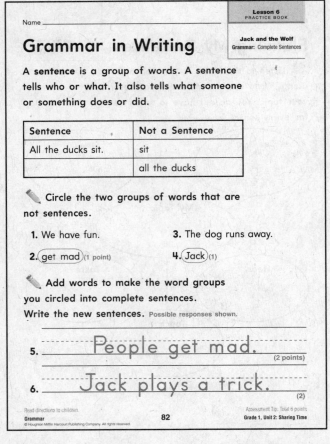

1. g **r** i n (1 point)

2. t **r** i m (1)

3. d **r** i p (1)

4. c **r** i b (1)

5. t **r** i p (1)

6. b **r** i m (1)

Lesson 7
PRACTICE BOOK

How Animals Communicate
Phonics: Clusters with r

Clusters with *r*

✏️ Name each picture. Circle the letters that stand for the beginning sounds. Write the letters to make the word.

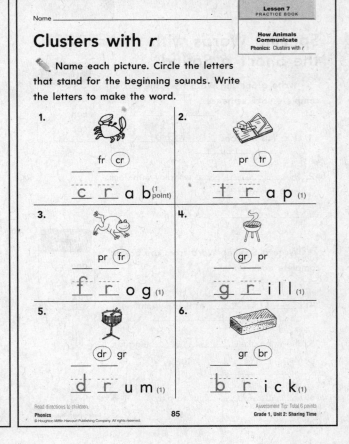

1. fr (cr)
c **r** a b (1 point)

2. pr (tr)
t **r** a p (1)

3. pr (fr)
f **r** o g (1)

4. (gr) pr
g **r** i l l (1)

5. (dr) gr
d **r** u m (1)

6. gr (br)
b **r** i c k (1)

Lesson 7
PRACTICE BOOK

How Animals
Communicate
Spelling: Words with
Short *i*

Spelling Words with the Short *i* Sound

Sort the words. Write the correct Spelling Words in each column.

Spelling Words

in
will
did
sit
six
big

Words that begin with a vowel	Words that begin with a consonant
in (1 point)	will (1)
	did (1)
	sit (1)
	six (1)
	big (1)

The Naming Part

Circle the subject, or naming part, in each sentence.

1. (Dogs) run. (1 point)

2. (The ants) make a nest. (1)

3. (The cat) comes to me. (1)

4. (The ducks) peck. (1)

5. (A bull) kicks. (1)

6. (The bug) makes a web. (1)

7. (The pigs) play in the mud. (1)

8. (A fox) sits on a log. (1)

Adjectives

Draw a picture of an animal doing something.

Word Bank

big
small
slow
loud
quiet
soft
young

Listen to the adjectives in the Word Bank. Read along. Complete each sentence with a word from the Word Bank or your own adjective. Possible responses shown.

1. The animal is ___small___ . (1 point)

2. The animal is ___hungry___ . (1)

3. The animal is ___soft___ . (1)

4. The animal is ___friendly___ . (1)

Short *i* and Clusters with *r*

Write words that rhyme. Use the words in the box.

trick grab dress drill grass quit tracks truck

1. brick	trick (1 point)	2. grill	drill (1)
3. press	dress (1)	4. crab	grab (1)
5. cracks	tracks (1)	6. duck	truck (1)
7. sit	quit (1)	8. brass	grass (1)

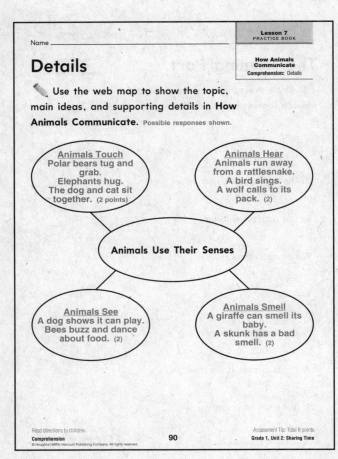

Name _____

Lesson 7
PRACTICE BOOK

How Animals
Communicate
Comprehension: Details

Details

✎ Use the web map to show the topic, main ideas, and supporting details in **How Animals Communicate.** Possible responses shown.

Animals Touch
Polar bears tug and grab.
Elephants hug.
The dog and cat sit together. (2 points)

Animals Hear
Animals run away from a rattlesnake.
A bird sings.
A wolf calls to its pack. (2)

Animals Use Their Senses

Animals See
A dog shows it can play.
Bees buzz and dance about food. (2)

Animals Smell
A giraffe can smell its baby.
A skunk has a bad smell. (2)

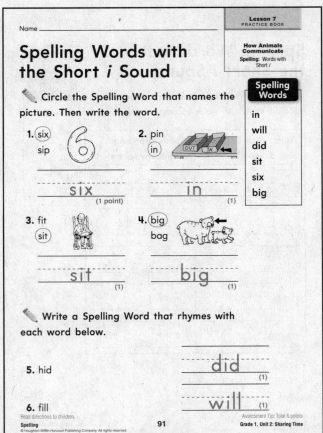

Name _____

Lesson 7
PRACTICE BOOK

How Animals
Communicate
Spelling: Words with Short i

Spelling Words with the Short *i* Sound

✎ Circle the Spelling Word that names the picture. Then write the word.

Spelling Words

in
will
did
sit
six
big

1. six
   sip

six
(1 point)

2. pin
   in

in
(1)

3. fit
   sit

sit
(1)

4. big
   bag

big
(1)

✎ Write a Spelling Word that rhymes with each word below.

5. hid

did
(1)

6. fill

will
(1)

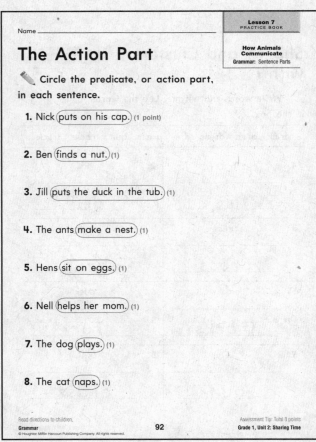

Name _____

Lesson 7
PRACTICE BOOK

How Animals
Communicate
Grammar: Sentence Parts

The Action Part

✎ Circle the predicate, or action part, in each sentence.

1. Nick (puts on his cap.) (1 point)

2. Ben (finds a nut.) (1)

3. Jill (puts the duck in the tub.) (1)

4. The ants (make a nest.) (1)

5. Hens (sit on eggs.) (1)

6. Nell (helps her mom.) (1)

7. The dog (plays.) (1)

8. The cat (naps.) (1)

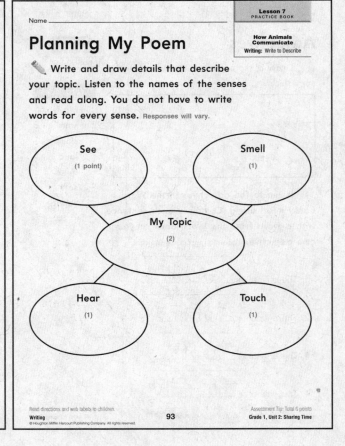

Name _____

Lesson 7
PRACTICE BOOK

How Animals
Communicate
Writing: Write to Describe

Planning My Poem

✎ Write and draw details that describe your topic. Listen to the names of the senses and read along. You do not have to write words for every sense. Responses will vary.

See
(1 point)

Smell
(1)

My Topic
(2)

Hear
(1)

Touch
(1)

Spelling Words with the Short *i* Sound

✏️ Write the correct word to complete each sentence.

1. I have a _____ **big** _____ dog. (big, bag)
   (1 point)

2. _____ **Did** _____ you see my mat? (Dad, Did)
   (1)

3. Jon will _____ **sit** _____ down. (sit, sat)
   (1)

4. _____ **Will** _____ you help me with the cats? (Wall, Will)
   (1)

5. I put the hat _____ **in** _____ my bag. (in, an)
   (1)

6. The hen has _____ **six** _____ eggs. (mix, six)
   (1)

Spiral Review

✏️ Listen to the nouns in the Word Bank. Read along. Write a noun from the box to name each picture.

Word Bank
web
pond
nest
bowl

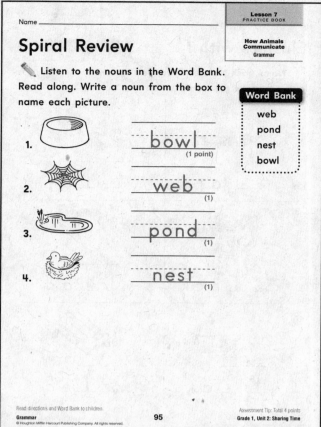

1. _____ **bowl** _____
   (1 point)

2. _____ **web** _____
   (1)

3. _____ **pond** _____
   (1)

4. _____ **nest** _____
   (1)

Grammar in Writing

Every sentence has two parts. The naming part is called the **subject**. The action part is called the **predicate**.

Example: The dogs bark loudly.
      subject   predicate

✏️ Circle the two groups of words that are not sentences.

1. The fox plays.

2. (The kittens) (1 point)

3. A pig sits in the mud.

4. (look for food) (1)

✏️ Add words to make the word groups you circled into complete sentences.

Possible responses shown.

5. _____ **The kittens play.** _____
   (2 points)

6. _____ **The bears look for food.** _____
   (2)

Words to Know

✏️ Choose the word that fits best in the sentence. Write the word on the line.

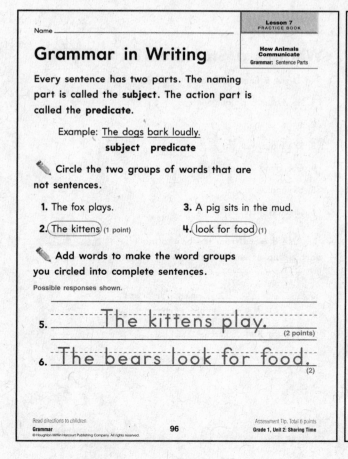

1. Jen will fix (her, she, today) bed. _____ **her** _____
   (1 point)

2. I (our, here, would) like to help. _____ **would** _____
   (1)

3. (Her, Now, She) is my friend. _____ **She** _____
   (1)

4. We have a lot to do (our, today, she). _____ **today** _____
   (1)

5. We did (she, here, our) job! _____ **our** _____
   (1)

6. We can play (our, now, her). _____ **now** _____
   (1)

Clusters with *l*

✏️ Name each picture. Write the first two letters to make the word.

1. p l a t e
   (1 point)

2. p l a y
   (1)

3. b l o c k
   (1)

4. g l a d
   (1)

5. f l a t
   (1)

6. s l e d
   (1)

Clusters with *l*

✏️ Circle the word to finish the sentence. Write the word.

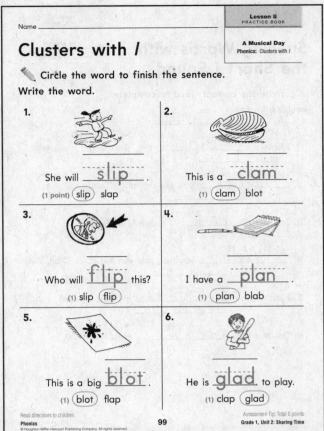

1. She will ___slip___ .
   (1 point) (slip) slap

2. This is a ___clam___ .
   (1) (clam) blot

3. Who will ___flip___ this?
   (1) slip (flip)

4. I have a ___plan___ .
   (1) (plan) blab

5. This is a big ___blot___ .
   (1) (blot) flap

6. He is ___glad___ to play.
   (1) clap (glad)

Spelling Words with the Short *o* Sound

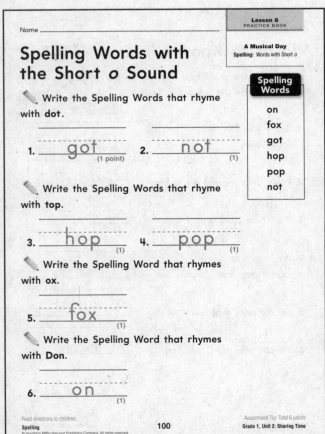

Spelling Words
on
fox
got
hop
pop
not

✏️ Write the Spelling Words that rhyme with dot.

1. ___got___
   (1 point)

2. ___not___
   (1)

✏️ Write the Spelling Words that rhyme with top.

3. ___hop___
   (1)

4. ___pop___
   (1)

✏️ Write the Spelling Word that rhymes with ox.

5. ___fox___
   (1)

✏️ Write the Spelling Word that rhymes with Don.

6. ___on___
   (1)

What Is a Statement?

✏️ Draw a line under each statement.

1. He makes a drum. (1 point)
2. sings
3. She plays well. (1)
4. Our band will win. (1)
5. Bill and Sam
6. Nick claps for us. (1)

✏️ Use a word from the box to make each group of words a statement.

Word Bank
listen
Meg

7. ___Meg___ plays the drums.
   (2)

8. Ken and Kim ___listen___
   (2)

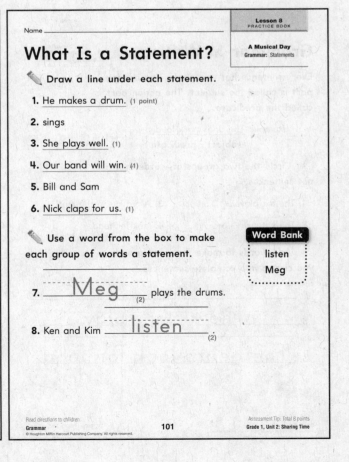

Name _____

Using Exact Adjectives

🖊 Fill in the blanks in the draft of the thank-you note. Listen to the adjectives in the Word Bank. Read along. Choose adjectives from the box. Write your own words, too. **Responses will vary.**

Word Bank

hot	huge	icy	tall	round
soft	striped	sweet	green	yellow

_____

Dear (1 point) _____ ,

Thank you for the (2) _____

_____ . It is (2) _____

_____ . I like the _____

(2) _____

102

Short *i* and Clusters with *l*

🖊 Name each picture. Circle the letters that stand for the beginning sounds. Write the word.

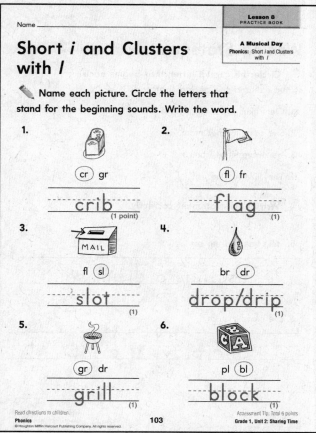

1. (cr) gr

crib
(1 point)

2. (fl) fr

flag
(1)

3. fl (sl)

slot
(1)

4. br (dr)

drop/drip
(1)

5. (gr) dr

grill
(1)

6. pl (bl)

block
(1)

103

Sequence of Events

🖊 Use the chart to tell the sequence of events in the story.

First

First, Mom and Dad go away and Aunt Viv comes. (2 points)

↓

Next

Next, Aunt Viv and the children make instruments. (2)

↓

Last

Last, they play music together. (2)

104

Spelling Words with the Short *o* Sound

🖊 Write the missing letter to complete each Spelling Word. Then write the word.

Spelling Words

on
got
fox
hop
pop
not

1. f _o_ x

fox
(1 point)

2. n _o_ t

not
(1)

3. p _o_ p

pop
(1)

4. h _o_ p

hop
(1)

5. _o_ n

on
(1)

6. g _o_ t

got
(1)

105

Writing Statements

✏️ Circle the capital letter that begins each statement and the period that ends it.

1. (C)lem likes my song(.) (2 points)

2. (S)he sings for her mom(.) (2)

3. (H)er mom sings, too(.) (2)

4. (T)hey like to sing(.) (2)

✏️ Write each statement correctly.

5. tess has a drum set

    Tess has a drum set. (3)

6. she plays it a lot

    She plays it a lot. (3)

Planning My Thank-You Note

Responses will vary.

I will write my thank-you note to

_____

(1 point) _____ .

✏️ Draw a picture of what you are thankful for. Write some details for your note.

(1 point) _____

I am thankful for (1) _____

(1) _____

(1) _____

(1) _____

Spelling Words with the Short o Sound

✏️ Write a Spelling Word to complete each sentence.

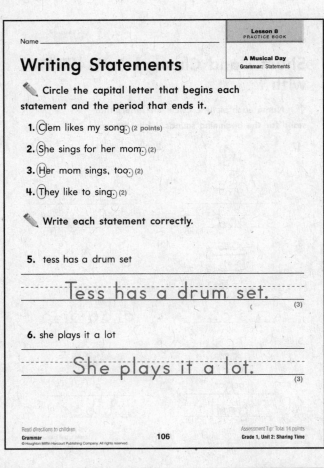

Spelling Words

on
fox
got
pop
not
hop

1. This animal is a ___fox___ . (1 point)

2. I ___got___ a dog from Bob. (1)

3. I like caps but ___not___ hats. (1)

4. The bag will ___pop___ if you fill it up. (1)

5. The fox will ___hop___ off the box. (1)

6. Do not sit ___on___ the bed. (1)

Spiral Review

✏️ Listen to the verbs in the Word Bank. Read along. Write a verb from the box to name each action.

Word Bank

play
dance
sing
watch

1.  ___dance___ (1 point)

2. ___sing___ (1)

3. ___play___ (1)

4. ___watch___ (1)

Lesson 8
PRACTICE BOOK

Name _____

Grammar in Writing

A Musical Day
Grammar: Statements

A statement begins with a **capital letter** and ends with a **period**.

✎ Fix the mistakes in these statements. Use proofreading marks.

Example: we play the bells ∧

1. she hits a big drum (2 points)

2. he holds a doll (2)

3. they have big hats (2)

4. we tap and sing (2)

Proofreading Marks	
∧	add
≡	capital letter

Read directions to children.
Grammar
© Houghton Mifflin Harcourt Publishing Company. All rights reserved.
110
Assessment Tip: Total 8 points
Grade 1, Unit 2: Sharing Time

Lesson 9
PRACTICE BOOK

Name _____

Words to Know

Dr. Seuss
High-Frequency Words

This is my cat.

✎ Circle the word that fits in each sentence. Write that word on the line.

1. I like to (read) after, was).

_____read_____ (1 point)

2. The cat (after, was, draw) in his bed.

_____was_____ (1)

3. I like to (after, was, draw) animals.

_____draw_____ (1)

4. Here are (writes, pictures, reads) of my cat.

_____pictures_____ (1)

5. Now I will (was, after, write) to my dad.

_____write_____ (1)

6. I will help you (after, draw, read) I call Brad.

_____after_____ (1)

Read directions to children.
High-Frequency Words
© Houghton Mifflin Harcourt Publishing Company. All rights reserved.
111
Assessment Tip: Total 6 points
Grade 1, Unit 2: Sharing Time

Lesson 9
PRACTICE BOOK

Name _____

Clusters with *s*

Dr. Seuss
Phonics: Clusters with s

✎ Name each picture. Write the first two or three letters that stand for the beginning sounds. Use the letters from the box.

st	sw	sn	sk	str

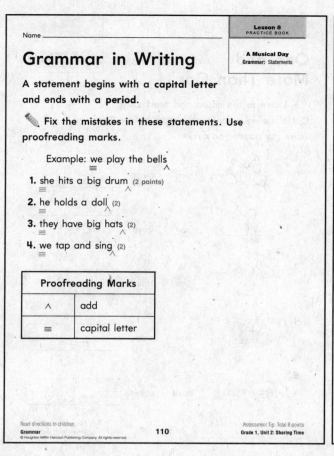

1. _____sn_____ (1 point)

2. _____sw_____ (1)

3. _____st_____ (1)

4. _____str_____ (1)

5. _____sk_____ (1)

Read directions to children.
Phonics
© Houghton Mifflin Harcourt Publishing Company. All rights reserved.
112
Assessment Tip: Total 5 points
Grade 1, Unit 2: Sharing Time

Lesson 9
PRACTICE BOOK

Name _____

Clusters with *s*

Dr. Seuss
Phonics: Clusters with s

✎ Circle the word that finishes the sentence. Write the word.

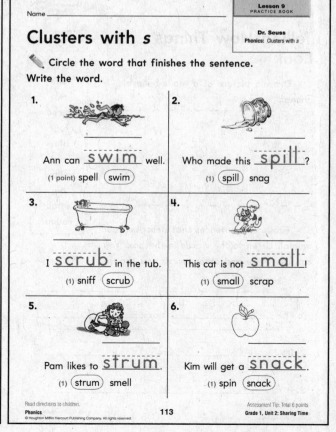

1. Ann can _____swim_____ well.
(1 point) spell (swim)

2. Who made this _____spill_____?
(1) (spill) snag

3. I _____scrub_____ in the tub.
(1) sniff (scrub)

4. This cat is not _____small_____!
(1) (small) scrap

5. Pam likes to _____strum_____.
(1) (strum) smell

6. Kim will get a _____snack_____.
(1) spin (snack)

Read directions to children.
Phonics
© Houghton Mifflin Harcourt Publishing Company. All rights reserved.
113
Assessment Tip: Total 6 points
Grade 1, Unit 2: Sharing Time

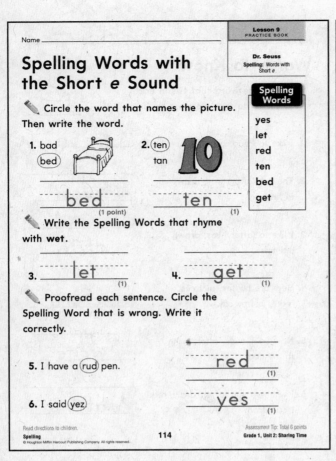

Name _____

Spelling Words with the Short *e* Sound

✏️ Circle the word that names the picture. Then write the word.

Spelling Words

yes
let
red
ten
bed
get

1. bad
   (bed)

   _b e d_
   (1 point)

2. (ten)
   tan

   10

   _t e n_
   (1)

✏️ Write the Spelling Words that rhyme with **wet**.

3. _l e t_
   (1)

4. _g e t_
   (1)

✏️ Proofread each sentence. Circle the Spelling Word that is wrong. Write it correctly.

5. I have a (rud) pen.

   _r e d_
   (1)

6. I said (yez)

   _y e s_
   (1)

114

Name _____

One and More Than One

✏️ Listen to the nouns and read along. Circle the noun for each picture below. Then write the nouns you circled.

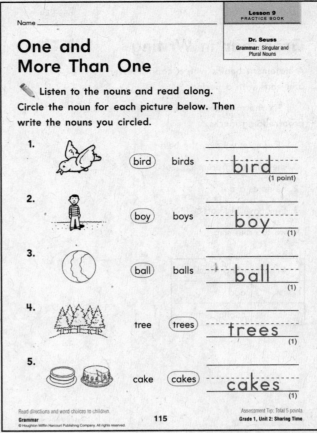

1. (bird) birds

   bird
   (1 point)

2. (boy) boys

   boy
   (1)

3. (ball) balls

   ball
   (1)

4. tree (trees)

   trees
   (1)

5. cake (cakes)

   cakes
   (1)

115

Name _____

Telling How Things Look

🖍️ Draw a picture of a make-believe animal.

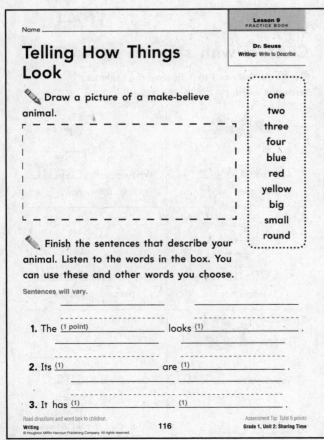

**one
two
three
four
blue
red
yellow
big
small
round**

✏️ Finish the sentences that describe your animal. Listen to the words in the box. You can use these and other words you choose.

Sentences will vary.

1. The (1 point) _____ looks (1) _____

2. Its (1) _____ are (1) _____

3. It has (1) _____ (1) _____

116

Name _____

Short *e* and Clusters with *s*

✏️ Name each picture. Circle the letters that stand for the beginning sounds. Write the letters. Write the word.

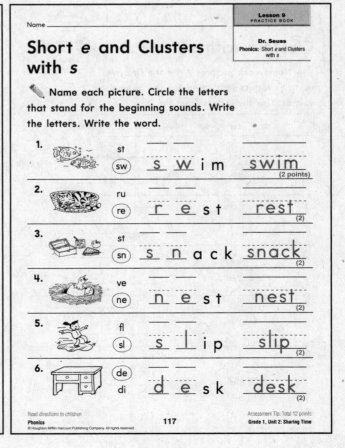

1. st
   (sw)

   _s w_ i m   _swim_
   (2 points)

2. ru
   (re)

   _r e_ s t   _rest_
   (2)

3. st
   (sn)

   _s n_ a c k   _snack_
   (2)

4. ve
   (ne)

   _n e_ s t   _nest_
   (2)

5. fl
   (sl)

   _s l_ i p   _slip_
   (2)

6. (de)
   di

   _d e_ s k   _desk_
   (2)

117

Text and Graphic Features

✏ Use the chart to list the story features and their purposes.

Feature	Purpose
Children may list any of the following:	
Photograph on p. 124	shows what Dr. Seuss looked like
Photograph on p. 125	shows that Ted was a funny man
Photograph on p. 126	shows Ted at work
Illustration on p. 127	show Ted's artwork
Photographs on pp. 129–130	show some of the books that Ted wrote
Art on pp. 132–133	shows some of the rhyming words Ted used in his stories
Photographs on pp. 134–135	show how popular Dr. Seuss's animal characters are
Photograph on p. 136	supports the author's statement that kids still read Dr. Seuss
(4 points)	(4)

Read directions to children.
Comprehension
© Houghton Mifflin Harcourt Publishing Company. All rights reserved.
118
Assessment Tip: Total 8 points
Grade 1, Unit 2: Sharing Time

Spelling Words with the Short *e* Sound

✏ Write the Spelling Words in ABC order.

1. __bed__ (1 point)
2. __get__ (1)
3. __let__ (1)
4. __red__ (1)
5. __ten__ (1)
6. __yes__ (1)

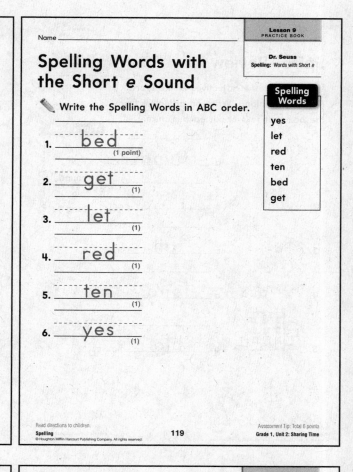

Spelling Words

yes
let
red
ten
bed
get

Read directions to children.
Spelling
© Houghton Mifflin Harcourt Publishing Company. All rights reserved.
119
Assessment Tip: Total 6 points
Grade 1, Unit 2: Sharing Time

Special Plural Nouns

✏ Listen to the nouns and read along. Circle the noun for each picture below. Then write the nouns you circled.

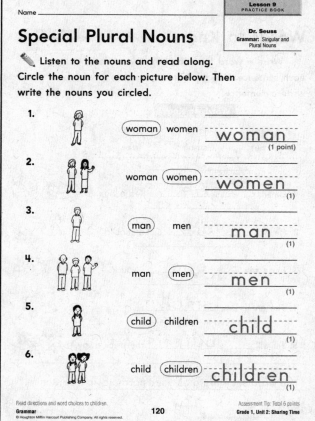

1. (woman) women __woman__ (1 point)
2. woman (women) __women__ (1)
3. (man) men __man__ (1)
4. man (men) __men__ (1)
5. (child) children __child__ (1)
6. child (children) __children__ (1)

Read directions and word choices to children.
Grammar
© Houghton Mifflin Harcourt Publishing Company. All rights reserved.
120
Assessment Tip: Total 6 points
Grade 1, Unit 2: Sharing Time

Spelling Words with the Short *e* Sound

✏ Write a Spelling Word to complete each sentence.

1. Get out of __bed__ (1 point), Fred!
2. Will you __let__ (1) me in?
3. Ben has __ten__ (1) pet ducks.
4. Will you __get__ (1) that bug away from me?
5. __Yes__ (1), I will hop with you.
6. Jeff likes the __red__ (1) cap best.

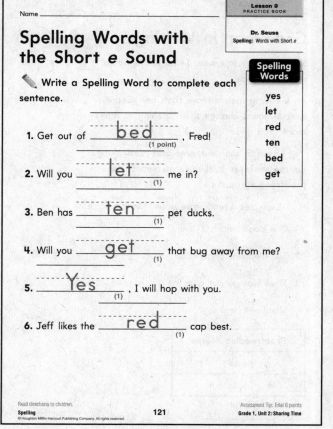

Spelling Words

yes
let
red
ten
bed
get

Read directions to children.
Spelling
© Houghton Mifflin Harcourt Publishing Company. All rights reserved.
121
Assessment Tip: Total 6 points
Grade 1, Unit 2: Sharing Time

Spiral Review

Name _____

✏️ Listen to the adjectives in the Word Bank. Read along. Write an adjective from the box that tells about each picture.

Word Bank
tiny
tall
round
big
long

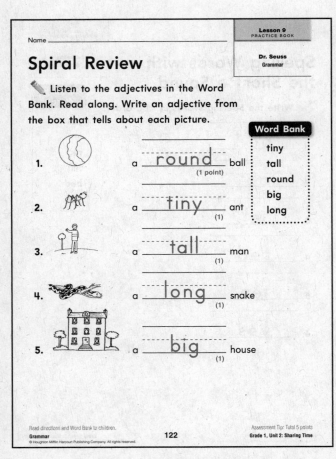

1. a __round__ ball
   (1 point)

2. a __tiny__ ant
   (1)

3. a __tall__ man
   (1)

4. a __long__ snake
   (1)

5. a __big__ house
   (1)

Planning My Description

Name _____

✏️ Listen to the labels in the web and read along. Write and draw details that tell size, shape, color, and number. Responses will vary.

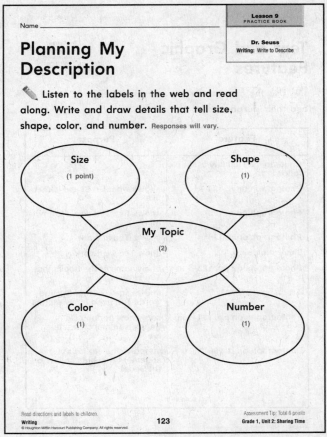

Size (1 point)

Shape (1)

My Topic (2)

Color (1)

Number (1)

Grammar in Writing

Name _____

Some **nouns** name one. Some nouns name more than one.

An **s** ending means more than one. Some special nouns change their spelling to name more than one.

✏️ Listen to the sentences and read along. Fix the mistakes in these statements. Use proofreading marks.

Examples: I read three ~~book~~. Two ~~man~~ talk.
                              books⌃   men⌃

1. One ~~dogs~~ swims. (2 points)
        dog⌃

2. Two ~~elephant~~ drink water. (2)
        elephants⌃

3. Three ~~woman~~ eat cake. (2)
          women⌃

4. Many ~~bell~~ ring. (2)
         bells⌃

Proofreading Marks	
⌃	add
✐	take out

Words to Know

Name _____

✏️ Write a word from the box to complete each sentence. Use the leftover word to write a sentence.

Words to Know
eat   give   one
put   small   take

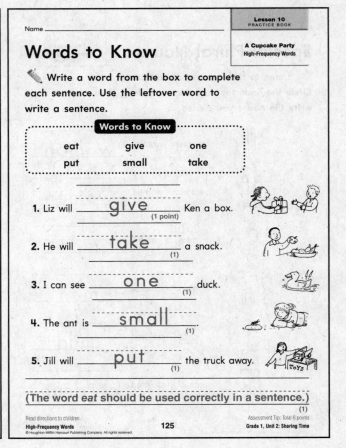

1. Liz will __give__ Ken a box.
   (1 point)

2. He will __take__ a snack.
   (1)

3. I can see __one__ duck.
   (1)

4. The ant is __small__.
   (1)

5. Jill will __put__ the truck away.
   (1)

(The word *eat* should be used correctly in a sentence.)
   (1)

Final Clusters

✏️ Name each picture. Write the letters that stand for the ending sounds. Use the letters from the box.

nd	mp	nt	st	sk

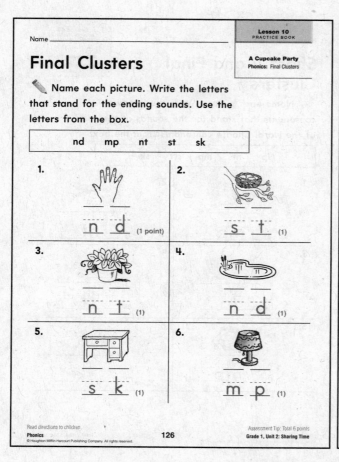

1. n d (1 point)

2. s t (1)

3. n t (1)

4. n d (1)

5. s k (1)

6. m p (1)

Read directions to children.
Phonics
© Houghton Mifflin Harcourt Publishing Company. All rights reserved.
126
Assessment Tip: Total 6 points
Grade 1, Unit 2: Sharing Time

Final Clusters

✏️ Name each picture. Circle the word to finish the sentence.

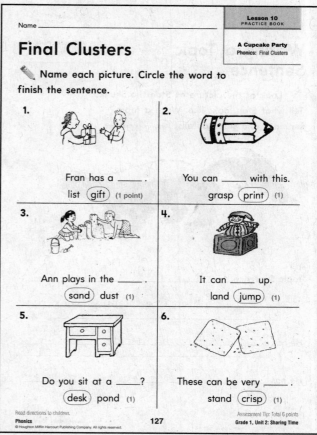

1. Fran has a _____.
   list (gift) (1 point)

2. You can _____ with this.
   grasp (print) (1)

3. Ann plays in the _____.
   (sand) dust (1)

4. It can _____ up.
   land (jump) (1)

5. Do you sit at a _____?
   (desk) pond (1)

6. These can be very _____.
   stand (crisp) (1)

Read directions to children.
Phonics
© Houghton Mifflin Harcourt Publishing Company. All rights reserved.
127
Assessment Tip: Total 6 points
Grade 1, Unit 2: Sharing Time

Spelling Words with the Short *u* Sound

Spelling Words
us
sun
but
fun
bus
run

✏️ Write the Spelling Words that end with **un**.

1. sun (1 point)

2. fun (1)

3. run (1)

✏️ Write the Spelling Words that end with **us**.

4. us (1)

5. bus (1)

✏️ Write the Spelling Word that ends with **ut**.

6. but (1)

Read directions to children.
Spelling
© Houghton Mifflin Harcourt Publishing Company. All rights reserved.
128
Assessment Tip: Total 6 points
Grade 1, Unit 2: Sharing Time

Prepositions for Where

✏️ Circle the preposition in each sentence. Write it on the line.

1. The gift was (in) a box.
   in (1 point)

2. Nan put it (on) a desk.
   on (1)

3. Some are (under) a bed.
   under (1)

4. The gift fell (off) the desk.
   off (1)

Complete each sentence. Write a preposition that tells where. Possible responses shown.

5. Nan went up the steps. (1)

6. She put Dan's gift on the desk. (1)

Read directions to children.
Grammar
© Houghton Mifflin Harcourt Publishing Company. All rights reserved.
129
Assessment Tip: Total 6 points
Grade 1, Unit 2: Sharing Time

Writing a Topic Sentence

✏️ Look at the picture of Stan the Skunk. Tell what Stan looks like. Write a topic sentence and some details. Responses will vary.

Topic Sentence: _____

Stan is a friendly skunk. (2 points)

He has a _____ white stripe _____ (1) .

He has _____ four legs _____ (1) .

Read directions to children.
Writing
© Houghton Mifflin Harcourt Publishing Company. All rights reserved.
130
Assessment Tip: Total 4 points
Grade 1, Unit 2: Sharing Time

Short *u* and Final Clusters

✏️ Name each picture. Write the last two consonants that stand for the sounds at the end of the word. Choose consonants from the box.

lp	nt	mp	ft	sk

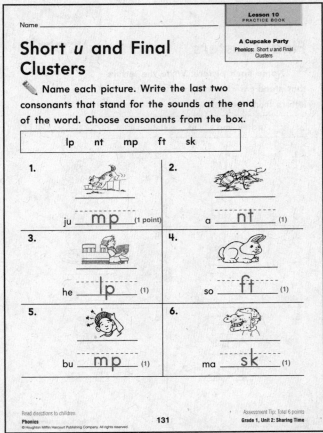

1. ju __mp__ (1 point)

2. a __nt__ (1)

3. he __lp__ (1)

4. so __ft__ (1)

5. bu __mp__ (1)

6. ma __sk__ (1)

Read directions to children.
Phonics
© Houghton Mifflin Harcourt Publishing Company. All rights reserved.
131
Assessment Tip: Total 6 points
Grade 1, Unit 2: Sharing Time

Story Structure

✏️ Use the Story Map to identify the characters, setting, and plot in the story.

Characters	Setting
Fritz, Kit, Jack, Fran, Stan, and Glen (2 points)	over several days in and around a chipmunk's home (2)

Plot

Fritz wakes up, misses his friends, and decides to have a big party.

Fritz invites five friends to the party. They all agree to come.

Fritz makes cupcakes with his friends' pictures on them.

Fritz's friends come to the party and give him a giant acorn.

Everyone eats and has fun. (6)

Read directions to children.
Comprehension
© Houghton Mifflin Harcourt Publishing Company. All rights reserved.
132
Assessment Tip: Total 10 points
Grade 1, Unit 2: Sharing Time

Spelling Words with the Short *u* Sound

✏️ Write the missing letter to complete each Spelling Word. Then write the word.

Spelling Words
us
sun
but
fun
bus
run

1. b __u__ t _____ but _____ (1 point)

2. s __u__ n _____ sun _____ (1)

3. __u__ s _____ us _____ (1)

4. f __u__ n _____ fun _____ (1)

5. b __u__ s _____ bus _____ (1)

6. r __u__ n _____ run _____ (1)

Read directions to children.
Spelling
© Houghton Mifflin Harcourt Publishing Company. All rights reserved.
133
Assessment Tip: Total 6 points
Grade 1, Unit 2: Sharing Time

Prepositions for When

✏️ Listen to the prepositions in the word box.
Read along. Circle the preposition in each sentence.
Write it on the line.

during	at	after	before

1. Let us write (after) we read.   **after**
(1 point)

2. We will sing (during) class.   **during**
(1)

3. She will come back (before) you do.   **before**
(1)

Complete each sentence. Write a preposition
that tells when.

Possible responses shown.

4. I read **before** I go to bed.
(1)

5. We will go **at** six.
(1)

134

Spelling Words with the Short *u* Sound

✏️ Write a Spelling Word to complete
each sentence.

1. Here comes the **bus**.
(1 point)

2. The **sun** is up.
(1)

3. The dog can **run** fast.
(1)

✏️ Write the correct word to complete
each sentence.

4. Will you come with **us**?

us
is

5. We had a lot of **fun**.
(1)

fun
fan

6. I like black **but** not red.
(1)

bat
but

135

Spiral Review

✏️ Listen to the adjectives in the Word
Bank. Read along. Write an adjective from
the box that tells about each picture.

Word Bank
two
three
four

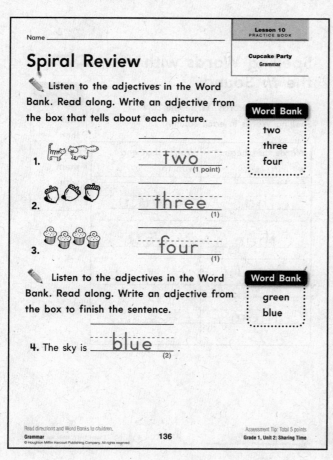

1. **two**
(1 point)

2. **three**
(1)

3. **four**
(1)

✏️ Listen to the adjectives in the Word
Bank. Read along. Write an adjective from
the box to finish the sentence.

Word Bank
green
blue

4. The sky is **blue**
(2)

136

Grammar in Writing

✏️ Write four sentences about the picture
with prepositions that tell where or when.
Draw a line under each preposition.

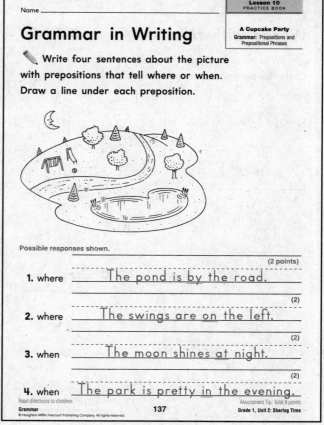

Possible responses shown.

(2 points)

1. where   The pond is by the road.
(2)

2. where   The swings are on the left.
(2)

3. when   The moon shines at night.
(2)

4. when   The park is pretty in the evening.

137

Words to Know

✏️ Listen to the riddles. Read along.
Circle the best answer to each riddle.

1. This is a place that is not near. (far)   where   live
   (1 point)

2. This is how snow feels.   their   blue   (cold)
   (1)

3. This word could start a question.   far   (where)   live
   (1)

4. A rock does not do this.   cold   where   (live)
   (1)

5. Rain is made of this.   (water)   far   cold
   (1)

6. The sky is this.   where   (blue)   little
   (1)

7. This is not big.   water   (little)   far
   (1)

8. This belongs to more than one person.   (their)   water   far
   (1)

Read directions and riddles to children
High-Frequency Words
© Houghton Mifflin Harcourt Publishing Company. All rights reserved.
138
Assessment Tip: Total 8 points
Grade 1, Unit 3: Nature Near and Far

Words with *th*

✏️ Circle the word that matches the picture.

1. wind   (with) (1 point)

2. tan   (thin)   (1)

3. (them)   ten   (1)

4. bat   (bath)   (1)

5. (path)   pet   (1)

6. kick   (thick)   (1)

Read directions to children.
Phonics
© Houghton Mifflin Harcourt Publishing Company. All rights reserved.
139
Assessment Tip: Total 6 points
Grade 1, Unit 3: Nature Near and Far

Words with *th*

✏️ Write th to finish the word and read it.
Circle the picture that matches the word.

1. m a t h
   (1 point)

2. t h i n k (1)

3. t h i c k (1)

4. b a t h (1)

5. t h i s (1)

Read directions to children.
Phonics
© Houghton Mifflin Harcourt Publishing Company. All rights reserved.
140
Assessment Tip: Total 5 points
Grade 1, Unit 3: Nature Near and Far

Spelling Words with the *th* Sound

✏️ Sort the words. Write the correct Spelling Words in each column.

Spelling Words

that
then
this
them
with
bath

Words that begin with th	Words that end with th
that (1 point)	with (1)
then (1)	bath (1)
this (1)	
them (1)	

Read directions to children.
Spelling
© Houghton Mifflin Harcourt Publishing Company. All rights reserved.
141
Assessment Tip: Total 6 points
Grade 1, Unit 3: Nature Near and Far

Names for People and Animals

✏️ Circle each proper noun that names a special person or animal.

1. My friend (Kim) sees a crab. (1 point)

2. (Stan Bock) sees it, too. (2)

3. They call the crab (Fred). (1)

✏️ Draw a line under each proper noun that names a special person or animal. Then write the proper noun correctly.

4. ann smith jumps into the water.

_____ Ann Smith _____ (2)

5. Her friend fran sees a crab with spots.

_____ Fran _____ (1)

6. She calls the crab spots.

_____ Spots _____ (1)

142

Assessment Tip: Total 8 points
Grade 1, Unit 3: Nature Near and Far

Words That Tell How

✏️ Draw a sea animal.

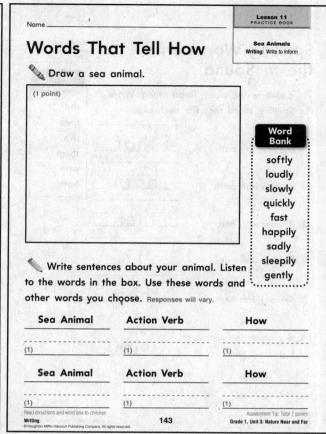

(1 point)

Word Bank

softly
loudly
slowly
quickly
fast
happily
sadly
sleepily
gently

✏️ Write sentences about your animal. Listen to the words in the box. Use these words and other words you choose. Responses will vary.

Sea Animal	Action Verb	How
(1)	(1)	(1)
Sea Animal	**Action Verb**	**How**
(1)	(1)	(1)

143

Assessment Tip: Total 7 points
Grade 1, Unit 3: Nature Near and Far

Base Words and -s, -es, -ed, -ing

✏️ Read the sentences. Circle the sentence that tells about the picture.

1. (The cat jumped.)

   The cat sat. (1 point)

2. He is helping.

   (He is resting.) (1)

3. (She packed a bag.)

   She pulled a bag. (1)

4. (Meg calls her pet.)

   Meg pets her cat. (1)

5. Val is drawing.

   (Val is looking.) (1)

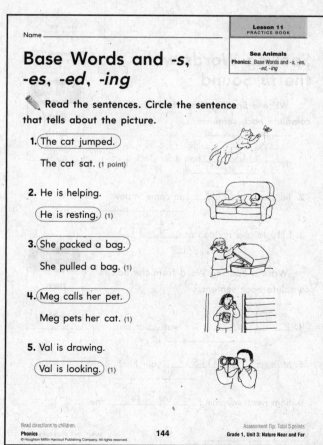

144

Assessment Tip: Total 5 points
Grade 1, Unit 3: Nature Near and Far

Author's Purpose

✏️ Think about why the author wrote Sea Animals. Then write the author's purpose and three details that tell about the purpose. Possible responses shown.

Detail	Detail	Detail
Sea animals are big and little. (1 point)	Some live in water and some on land. (1)	Some live where it is cold and some where it is warm. (1)

Purpose

The author wants to tell people about all the different animals that live in the sea. (1)

145

Assessment Tip: Total 4 points
Grade 1, Unit 3: Nature Near and Far

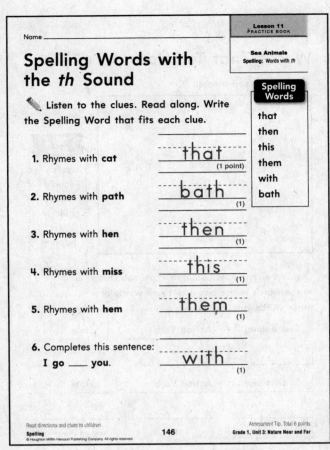

Spelling Words with the *th* Sound

✎ Listen to the clues. Read along. Write the Spelling Word that fits each clue.

Spelling Words
that
then
this
them
with
bath

1. Rhymes with **cat** _____that_____ (1 point)

2. Rhymes with **path** _____bath_____ (1)

3. Rhymes with **hen** _____then_____ (1)

4. Rhymes with **miss** _____this_____ (1)

5. Rhymes with **hem** _____them_____ (1)

6. Completes this sentence:
I go ___ you. _____with_____ (1)

Read directions and clues to children.
Spelling
© Houghton Mifflin Harcourt Publishing Company. All rights reserved.
146
Assessment Tip: Total 6 points
Grade 1, Unit 3: Nature Near and Far

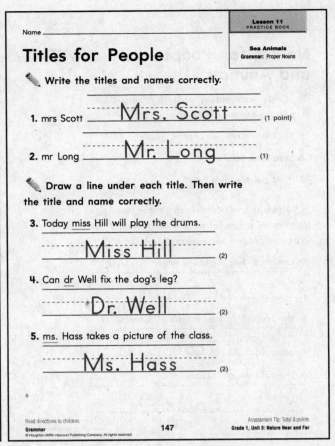

Titles for People

✎ Write the titles and names correctly.

1. mrs Scott _____Mrs. Scott_____ (1 point)

2. mr Long _____Mr. Long_____ (1)

✎ Draw a line under each title. Then write the title and name correctly.

3. Today miss Hill will play the drums.
_____Miss Hill_____ (2)

4. Can dr Well fix the dog's leg?
_____Dr. Well_____ (2)

5. ms. Hass takes a picture of the class.
_____Ms. Hass_____ (2)

Read directions to children.
Grammar
© Houghton Mifflin Harcourt Publishing Company. All rights reserved.
147
Assessment Tip: Total 8 points
Grade 1, Unit 3: Nature Near and Far

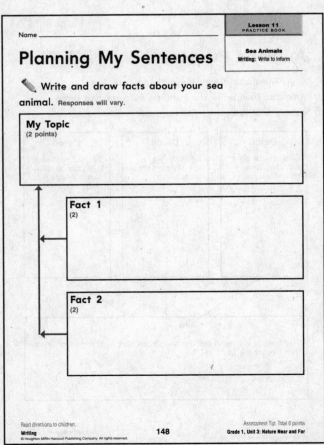

Planning My Sentences

✎ Write and draw facts about your sea animal. Responses will vary.

My Topic
(2 points)

Fact 1
(2)

Fact 2
(2)

Read directions to children.
Writing
© Houghton Mifflin Harcourt Publishing Company. All rights reserved.
148
Assessment Tip: Total 6 points
Grade 1, Unit 3: Nature Near and Far

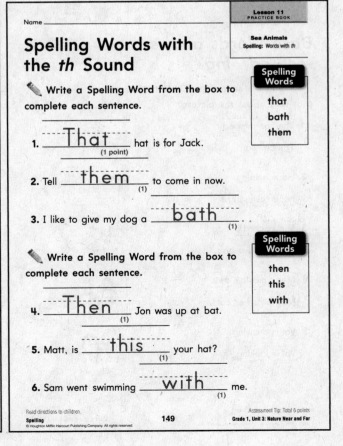

Spelling Words with the *th* Sound

✎ Write a Spelling Word from the box to complete each sentence.

Spelling Words
that
bath
them

1. _____That_____ hat is for Jack. (1 point)

2. Tell _____them_____ to come in now. (1)

3. I like to give my dog a _____bath_____ (1)

✎ Write a Spelling Word from the box to complete each sentence.

Spelling Words
then
this
with

4. _____Then_____ Jon was up at bat. (1)

5. Matt, is _____this_____ your hat? (1)

6. Sam went swimming _____with_____ me. (1)

Read directions to children.
Spelling
© Houghton Mifflin Harcourt Publishing Company. All rights reserved.
149
Assessment Tip: Total 6 points
Grade 1, Unit 3: Nature Near and Far

Spiral Review

🖊 Draw a line under each word group that is a sentence.

1. <u>The friends play tag.</u> (1 point)

2. digs in the sand

3. <u>The frog jumps up.</u> (1)

4. <u>Some kids look for crabs.</u> (1)

5. A red fox

🖊 Write a group of words from each word box to make a sentence.

| The crab | | a rock |
| This will | | rests on a rock |

6.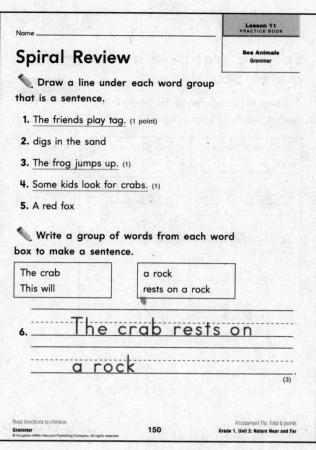
The crab rests on a rock

(3)

Read directions to children.
Grammar
© Houghton Mifflin Harcourt Publishing Company. All rights reserved.
150
Assessment Tip: Total 6 points
Grade 1, Unit 3: Nature Near and Far

Grammar in Writing

Nouns that name special people or animals are called **proper nouns**. Proper nouns begin with capital letters.

A **title** before a person's name begins with a capital letter. A title usually ends with a period.

🖊 Fix the mistakes in these statements. Use proofreading marks.

Examples: My fish is named gus.
I gave Mrs Billows a book.

1. My friend Dr Rudd helps animals. (2 points)

2. He has a pet crab called pinch. (2)

3. Our teacher, miss Land, reads about crabs. (2)

4. She gives the book to beth Bond. (2)

Proofreading Marks	
∧	add
≡	capital letter

Read directions to children.
Grammar
© Houghton Mifflin Harcourt Publishing Company. All rights reserved.
151
Assessment Tip: Total 8 points
Grade 1, Unit 3: Nature Near and Far

Words to Know

🖊 Circle the word that best completes each sentence.

1. The dog is (brown, very). (1 point)

2. Rich got the gift (been, out) of the box. (1)

3. I would like to have my (never, own) cat. (1)

4. Singing makes me (very, brown) happy. (1)

5. Have you (know, been) to the play? (1)

6. Do you (know, very) what to do next? (1)

7. Take (off, never) that hat. (1)

8. You (own, never) sing with me. (1)

Read directions to children.
High-Frequency Words
© Houghton Mifflin Harcourt Publishing Company. All rights reserved.
152
Assessment Tip: Total 8 points
Grade 1, Unit 3: Nature Near and Far

Words with *ch*, *tch*

🖊 Circle the word that matches the picture.

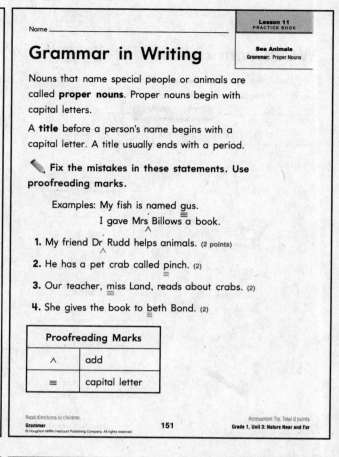

1. thick (chick) (1 point)

2. chip (champ) (1)

3. bend (bench) (1)

4. (hatch) hut (1)

5. (chin) check (1)

6. cats (catch) (1)

Read directions to children.
Phonics
© Houghton Mifflin Harcourt Publishing Company. All rights reserved.
153
Assessment Tip: Total 6 points
Grade 1, Unit 3: Nature Near and Far

Name _____

Lesson 12
PRACTICE BOOK

How Leopard Got
His Spots
Phonics: Words with *ch, tch*

Words with *ch*, *tch*

✏️ Read the words in the box. Write the word that matches the picture.

```
┄┄┄┄┄┄┄┄ Word Bank ┄┄┄┄┄┄┄┄
   lunch   check   chimp   chop   match
```

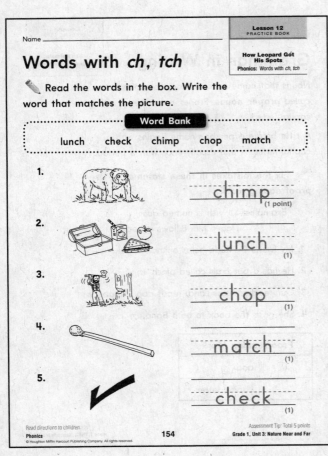

1. **chimp** (1 point)

2. **lunch** (1)

3. **chop** (1)

4. **match** (1)

5. **check** (1)

Read directions to children.
Phonics
© Houghton Mifflin Harcourt Publishing Company. All rights reserved.
154
Assessment Tip: Total 5 points
Grade 1, Unit 3: Nature Near and Far

Name _____

Lesson 12
PRACTICE BOOK

How Leopard Got
His Spots
Spelling: Words with *ch*

Spelling Words with the *ch* Sound

```
Spelling
Words

chin
chop
much
chip
rich
chick
```

✏️ Sort the words. Write the correct Spelling Words in each column.

Words that begin with ch	Words that end with ch
chin (1 point)	**much** (1)
chop (1)	**rich** (1)
chip (1)	
chick (1)	

Read directions to children.
Spelling
155
Assessment Tip: Total 6 points
Grade 1, Unit 3: Nature Near and Far
© Houghton Mifflin Harcourt Publishing Company. All rights reserved.

Name _____

Lesson 12
PRACTICE BOOK

How Leopard Got
His Spots
Grammar: Proper Nouns

Names of Places

✏️ Listen to some proper nouns in the Word Bank. Read along. Circle each proper noun that names a special place in the sentences.

```
┄┄┄┄┄┄┄ Word Bank ┄┄┄┄┄┄┄
  Street   Avenue   Park   Lake   School
```

1. There are many animals in (Red Fox Park.) (2 points)

2. I live on (Mint Avenue.) (2)

3. It is near (Elk Street.) (2)

✏️ Draw a line under each proper noun that names a special place. Then write the proper noun correctly.

4. We camp at elm lake.

   Elm Lake (2)

5. My friend lives on crab avenue.

   Crab Avenue (2)

Read directions to children.
Grammar
156
Assessment Tip: Total 10 points
Grade 1, Unit 3: Nature Near and Far
© Houghton Mifflin Harcourt Publishing Company. All rights reserved.

Name _____

Lesson 12
PRACTICE BOOK

How Leopard Got
His Spots
Writing: Write to Inform

Order Words

✏️ Write 1, 2, and 3 to put these pictures in order. (1 point for the correct order)

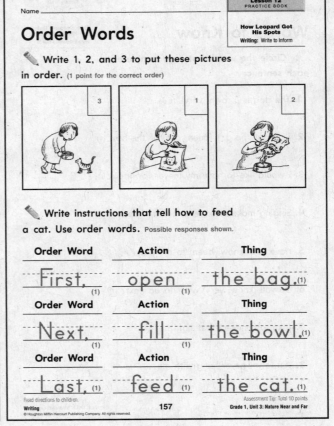

✏️ Write instructions that tell how to feed a cat. Use order words. Possible responses shown.

Order Word	Action	Thing
First, (1)	**open** (1)	**the bag.** (1)
Order Word	Action	Thing
Next, (1)	**fill** (1)	**the bowl.** (1)
Order Word	Action	Thing
Last, (1)	**feed** (1)	**the cat.** (1)

Read directions to children.
Writing
157
Assessment Tip: Total 10 points
Grade 1, Unit 3: Nature Near and Far
© Houghton Mifflin Harcourt Publishing Company. All rights reserved.

Name _____

Possessives with 's

✏️ Read the sentences. Circle the sentence
that tells about the picture.

1. (Mom's hat is off!) (1 point)

   Dad's hat is wet.

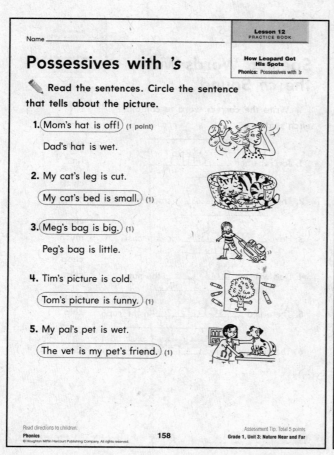

2. My cat's leg is cut.

   (My cat's bed is small.) (1)

3. (Meg's bag is big.) (1)

   Peg's bag is little.

4. Tim's picture is cold.

   (Tom's picture is funny.) (1)

5. My pal's pet is wet.

   (The vet is my pet's friend.) (1)

Read directions to children.
Phonics
© Houghton Mifflin Harcourt Publishing Company. All rights reserved.
158
Grade 1, Unit 3: Nature Near and Far
Assessment Tip: Total 5 points

Name _____

Sequence of Events

✏️ Use the chart to tell the sequence of
events in the story. Possible responses shown.

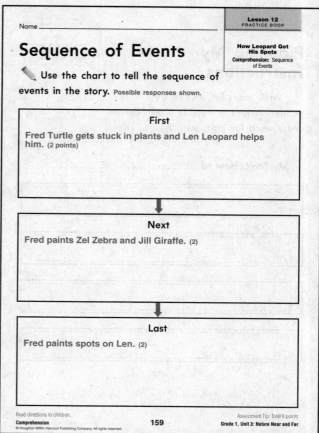

First
Fred Turtle gets stuck in plants and Len Leopard helps him. (2 points)

Next
Fred paints Zel Zebra and Jill Giraffe. (2)

Last
Fred paints spots on Len. (2)

Read directions to children.
Comprehension
© Houghton Mifflin Harcourt Publishing Company. All rights reserved.
159
Grade 1, Unit 3: Nature Near and Far
Assessment Tip: Total 6 points

Name _____

Spelling Words with ch

✏️ Listen to the clues. Read along. Write
the Spelling Word that fits each clue.

Spelling Words

chin
chop
much
chip
rich
chick

1. Opposite of **poor**   rich
   (1 point)

2. Rhymes with **hop**   chop
   (1)

3. Rhymes with **fin**   chin
   (1)

4. Opposite of **little**   much
   (1)

5. Rhymes with **hip**   chip
   (1)

6. Rhymes with **kick**   chick
   (1)

Read directions and clues to children.
Spelling
© Houghton Mifflin Harcourt Publishing Company. All rights reserved.
160
Grade 1, Unit 3: Nature Near and Far
Assessment Tip: Total 6 points

Name _____

More Place Names

✏️ Circle each proper noun that names
a special place.

1. Frank went to see Bill in (Kansas.) (2 points)

2. Bill just got back from (Canada.) (2)

✏️ Draw a line under each proper noun that names a
special place. Then write the proper noun correctly.

3. It is very cold in finland.

   Finland (2)

4. Meg lives in dallas.

   Dallas (2)

5. That is in texas.

   Texas (2)

Read directions to children.
Grammar
© Houghton Mifflin Harcourt Publishing Company. All rights reserved.
161
Grade 1, Unit 3: Nature Near and Far
Assessment Tip: Total 10 points

Name _____

Lesson 12
PRACTICE BOOK

How Leopard Got
His Spots
Writing: Write to Inform

Planning My Instructions

✏️ Write steps for making an animal puppet. Write the steps in order. Use an order word for each step. Responses will vary.

_____

My Topic: How to (1 point) _____

1. (1) _____

⬇️

2. (1) _____

⬇️

3. (1) _____

⬇️

4. (1) _____

Read directions to children.

Writing
© Houghton Mifflin Harcourt Publishing Company. All rights reserved.

162

Assessment Tip: Total 5 points

Grade 1, Unit 3: Nature Near and Far

Name _____

Lesson 12
PRACTICE BOOK

How Leopard Got
His Spots
Spelling: Words with ch

Spelling Words with the *ch* Sound

✏️ Write the correct word to complete each sentence.

1. Jan rubs her __chin__ (1 point) .

2. The __chick__ is small and soft. (1)

3. How __much__ does it cost? (1)

4. Dad will __chop__ the nuts. (1)

5. There is a __chip__ in the cup. (1)

6. The king was very __rich__ . (1)

chin	
fin	
chick	
check	
chum	
much	
chop	
chat	
ship	
chip	
rich	
rip	

Name _____

Lesson 12
PRACTICE BOOK

How Leopard Got
His Spots
Grammar

Spiral Review

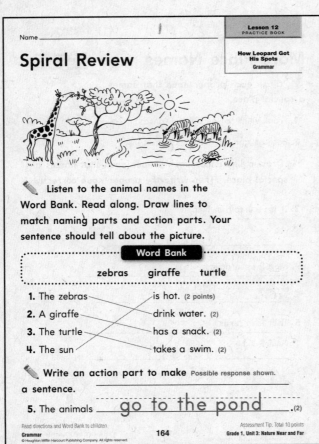

✏️ Listen to the animal names in the Word Bank. Read along. Draw lines to match naming parts and action parts. Your sentence should tell about the picture.

Word Bank
zebras   giraffe   turtle

1. The zebras —————— is hot. (2 points)
2. A giraffe —————— drink water. (2)
3. The turtle —————— has a snack. (2)
4. The sun —————— takes a swim. (2)

✏️ Write an action part to make **Possible response shown.** a sentence.

5. The animals __go to the pond__ . (2)

Read directions and Word Bank to children

Grammar
© Houghton Mifflin Harcourt Publishing Company. All rights reserved.

164

Assessment Tip: Total 10 points

Grade 1, Unit 3: Nature Near and Far

Name _____

Lesson 12
PRACTICE BOOK

How Leopard Got
His Spots
Grammar: Proper Nouns

Grammar in Writing

Proper nouns name special places. They begin with capital letters. Listen to the nouns in the Word Bank. Read along. Some of these can be both proper and common nouns, such as **road**.

Word Bank
America   School   Road   Canada

✏️ Fix the mistakes in these sentences. Use proofreading marks.

Example: We live in america.

1. I go to red plum school. (3 points)

2. I get on the bus at smith road. (2)

3. Liz wants to see the grand canyon. (2)

4. Have you been to canada? (1)

Proofreading Marks	
≡	capital letter

Words to Know

✏️ Circle the word that best completes each sentence.

1. Some frogs are ((green), grow). (1 point)

2. Let us have lunch (yellow, (down)) by the pond. (1)

3. It gets cold in the ((fall), new). (1)

4. My plants will (down, (grow)) well in the sun. (1)

5. Some of the buds are (goes, (open)). (1)

6. Do you like my ((new), down) hat? (1)

7. A big ((yellow), fall) truck will take the logs away. (1)

8. The truck (green, (goes)) to the dump. (1)

Read directions to children.
High-Frequency Words
© Houghton Mifflin Harcourt Publishing Company. All rights reserved.
166
Assessment Tip: Total 8 points
Grade 1, Unit 3: Nature Near and Far

Words with *sh*, *wh*, *ph*

✏️ Circle the word that matches the picture or belongs in the sentence.

1.
(shell) bell (1 point)

2.
_____ is this?
(What) Wish (1)

3.
_____ will he go?
Well (When) (1)

4.
bunch (brush) (1)

5.
(fish) fist (1)

6.
(Ralph) Jen (1)

Read directions to children.
Phonics
© Houghton Mifflin Harcourt Publishing Company. All rights reserved.
167
Assessment Tip: Total 6 points
Grade 1, Unit 3: Nature Near and Far

Words with *sh*, *wh*, *ph*

✏️ Circle the word that finishes the sentence. Then write the word on the line.

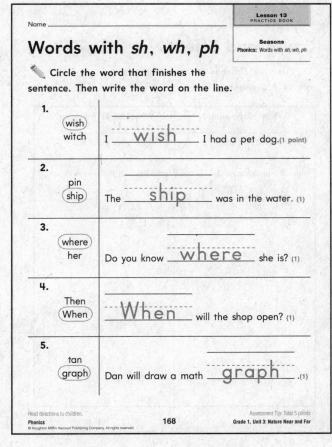

1.
(wish)
witch
I ___wish___ I had a pet dog. (1 point)

2.
pin
(ship)
The ___ship___ was in the water. (1)

3.
(where)
her
Do you know ___where___ she is? (1)

4.
Then
(When)
___When___ will the shop open? (1)

5.
tan
(graph)
Dan will draw a math ___graph___. (1)

Read directions to children.
Phonics
© Houghton Mifflin Harcourt Publishing Company. All rights reserved.
168
Assessment Tip: Total 5 points
Grade 1, Unit 3: Nature Near and Far

Spelling Words with the *sh* and *wh* Sounds

Spelling Words
ship
shop
which
when
whip
fish

✏️ Sort the words. Write the correct Spelling Words in each column.

Words with *sh*	Words with *wh*
ship (1 point)	which (1)
shop (1)	when (1)
fish (1)	whip (1)

✏️ Write two words that rhyme with **lip**.

ship (1)   whip (1)

Read directions to children.
Spelling
© Houghton Mifflin Harcourt Publishing Company. All rights reserved.
169
Assessment Tip: Total 8 points
Grade 1, Unit 3: Nature Near and Far

Subjects and Verbs

Name _____

Lesson 13
PRACTICE BOOK

Seasons
Grammar: Subjects
and Verbs

✏️ Write a verb from the box to tell what
the underlined subject is doing.

Word Bank
- picks
- hops
- sits
- runs
- comes

1. The <u>sun</u> __comes__ up. (2 points)

2. <u>Bev</u> __sits__ on the sand. (2)

3. <u>Tim</u> __picks__ up a stick. (2)

4. A <u>frog</u> __hops__ past. (2)

5. A <u>dog</u> __runs__ after the rabbits. (2)

Read directions to children.
Grammar
© Houghton Mifflin Harcourt Publishing Company. All rights reserved.
170
Assessment Tip: Total 10 points
Grade 1, Unit 3: Nature Near and Far

Main Idea

✏️ Write facts to finish three sentences
about a season. Then tell the main idea.

Topic Sentence _____
Here are some facts about (1 point) _____

Detail Sentence _____
_____
(1) _____ is a time when (2) _____
_____

Detail Sentence _____
The weather in (1) _____ gets
_____
(1) _____

Main Idea _____
All my sentences tell about (2) _____ .

Read directions to children.
Writing
© Houghton Mifflin Harcourt Publishing Company. All rights reserved.
171
Assessment Tip: Total 8 points
Grade 1, Unit 3: Nature Near and Far

Contractions with 's, n't

✏️ Draw a line from each pair of words to
its contraction.

can not   don't (1 point)

Let us   It's (1)

do not   can't (1)

It is   Let's (1)

Write the contraction from above that
finishes each sentence.

1. They __don't__ know what to do. (1)

2. __It's__ good to help a friend. (1)

3. __Let's__ go to see a play. (1)

4. He __can't__ find his hat. (1)

Read directions to children.
Phonics
© Houghton Mifflin Harcourt Publishing Company. All rights reserved.
172
Assessment Tip: Total 8 points
Grade 1, Unit 3: Nature Near and Far

Cause and Effect

✏️ Use the chart to tell about causes and
effects in **Seasons**.

What Happened?	Why Did It Happen?
buds began to grow	children planted seeds
chicks sing	eggs hatched
hear the grass squish (3 points)	grass is wet from rain (3)

Read directions to children.
Comprehension
© Houghton Mifflin Harcourt Publishing Company. All rights reserved.
173
Assessment Tip: Total 6 points
Grade 1, Unit 3: Nature Near and Far

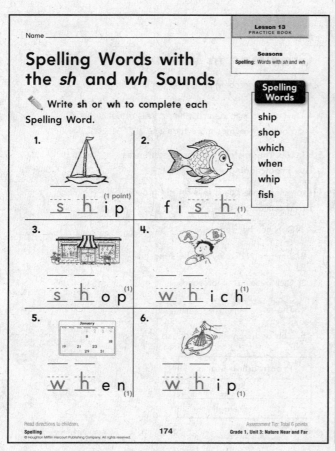

Spelling Words with the *sh* and *wh* Sounds

✏️ Write **sh** or **wh** to complete each Spelling Word.

Spelling Words

ship
shop
which
when
whip
fish

1. s h i p (1 point)

2. f i s h (1)

3. s h o p (1)

4. w h i c h (1)

5. w h e n (1)

6. w h i p (1)

Read directions to children.
Spelling
© Houghton Mifflin Harcourt Publishing Company. All rights reserved.
174
Assessment Tip: Total 6 points
Grade 1, Unit 3: Nature Near and Far

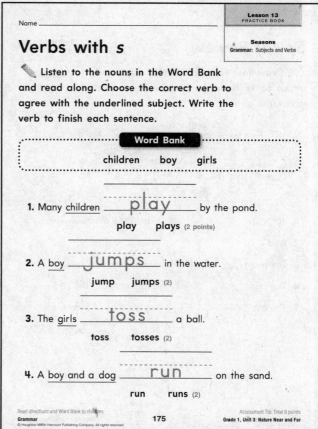

Verbs with *s*

✏️ Listen to the nouns in the Word Bank and read along. Choose the correct verb to agree with the underlined subject. Write the verb to finish each sentence.

Word Bank

children   boy   girls

1. Many <u>children</u> **play** by the pond.
   play   plays (2 points)

2. A <u>boy</u> **jumps** in the water.
   jump   jumps (2)

3. The <u>girls</u> **toss** a ball.
   toss   tosses (2)

4. A <u>boy</u> and a dog **run** on the sand.
   run   runs (2)

Read directions and Word Bank to children.
Grammar
© Houghton Mifflin Harcourt Publishing Company. All rights reserved.
175
Assessment Tip: Total 8 points
Grade 1, Unit 3: Nature Near and Far

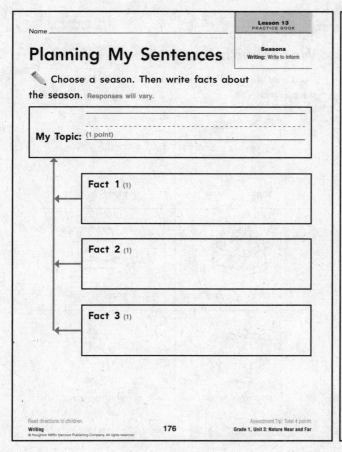

Planning My Sentences

✏️ Choose a season. Then write facts about the season. Responses will vary.

My Topic: (1 point)

Fact 1 (1)

Fact 2 (1)

Fact 3 (1)

Read directions to children.
Writing
© Houghton Mifflin Harcourt Publishing Company. All rights reserved.
176
Assessment Tip: Total 4 points
Grade 1, Unit 3: Nature Near and Far

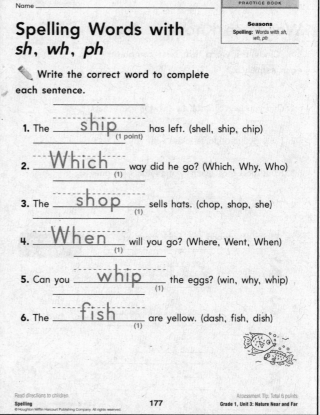

Spelling Words with *sh*, *wh*, *ph*

✏️ Write the correct word to complete each sentence.

1. The **ship** has left. (shell, ship, chip) (1 point)

2. **Which** way did he go? (Which, Why, Who) (1)

3. The **shop** sells hats. (chop, shop, she) (1)

4. **When** will you go? (Where, Went, When) (1)

5. Can you **whip** the eggs? (win, why, whip) (1)

6. The **fish** are yellow. (dash, fish, dish) (1)

Read directions to children.
Spelling
© Houghton Mifflin Harcourt Publishing Company. All rights reserved.
177
Assessment Tip: Total 6 points
Grade 1, Unit 3: Nature Near and Far

Spiral Review

✏️ Draw lines to match naming parts and action parts. Read the statements you made about the picture.

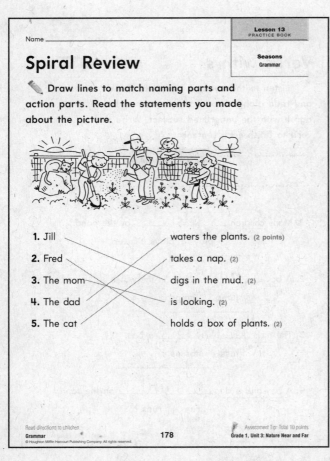

1. Jill
2. Fred
3. The mom
4. The dad
5. The cat

waters the plants. (2 points)
takes a nap. (2)
digs in the mud. (2)
is looking. (2)
holds a box of plants. (2)

Read directions to children.
Grammar
© Houghton Mifflin Harcourt Publishing Company. All rights reserved.
178
Assessment Tip: Total 10 points
Grade 1, Unit 3: Nature Near and Far

Name _____

Lesson 13
PRACTICE BOOK

Seasons
Grammar: Subjects
and Verbs

Grammar in Writing

- Add **s** to a **verb** when it tells about a noun that names one.
- Do not add **s** to a verb when it tells about a noun that names more than one.

✏️ Fix the mistakes in these sentences. Use proofreading marks.

Examples: Snowflakes ~~falls~~ fall on the ground.
David ~~put~~ puts on his coat.

1. Don ~~get~~ gets his sled. (2 points)
2. Jan and Nick plays play in the sand. (2)
3. Nick ~~make~~ makes a hill of sand. (2)
4. The dog jump jumps in the grass. (2)
5. Deb and Don ~~finds~~ find a cat. (2)

Proofreading Marks	
∧	add
⸌	take out

Read directions to children.
Grammar
© Houghton Mifflin Harcourt Publishing Company. All rights reserved.
179
Assessment Tip: Total 10 points
Grade 1, Unit 3: Nature Near and Far

Words to Know

✏️ Circle the word that best completes each sentence.

1. Can you (watch/into) my fish for me? (1 point)
2. I will go (into/starts) class with you. (1)
3. I am glad that lunch (watch/starts) at one. (1)
4. The fox jumps (over/watch) the log. (1)

✏️ Write the word for each number.

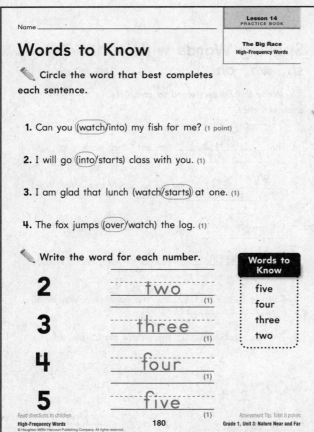

2   two (1)
3   three (1)
4   four (1)
5   five (1)

Words to Know
five
four
three
two

Read directions to children.
High-Frequency Words
© Houghton Mifflin Harcourt Publishing Company. All rights reserved.
180
Assessment Tip: Total 8 points
Grade 1, Unit 3: Nature Near and Far

Words with Long *a*

✏️ Circle the word that matches the picture.

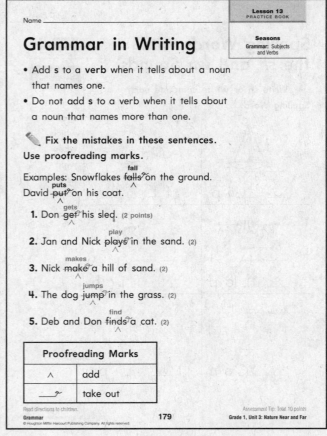

1. camp (crane) (1 point)
2. (plane) plan (1)
3. crack (cake) (1)
4. grass (gate) (1)
5. (whale) what (1)
6. vest (vase) (1)

Read directions to children.
Phonics
© Houghton Mifflin Harcourt Publishing Company. All rights reserved.
181
Assessment Tip: Total 6 points
Grade 1, Unit 3: Nature Near and Far

Name _____

Words with Long *a*

✏️ Write the word that goes with each clue.

Word Bank
plate
tape
male
skates
game
grape

1. You use this to close a box.
   <u>tape</u> (1 point)

2. A man is this.
   <u>male</u> (1)

3. You eat from this.
   <u>plate</u> (1)

4. Go fast on these.
   <u>skates</u> (1)

5. This is little and can be green.
   <u>grape</u> (1)

6. You play this with a friend.
   <u>game</u> (1)

Read directions to children.
Phonics
© Houghton Mifflin Harcourt Publishing Company. All rights reserved.
182
Assessment Tip: Total 6 points
Grade 1, Unit 3: Nature Near and Far

Spelling Words with the Long *a* Sound

✏️ Write the Spelling Words in ABC order.

Spelling Words
came
make
brave
late
gave
shape

1. <u>brave</u> (1 point)

2. <u>came</u> (1)

3. <u>gave</u> (1)

4. <u>late</u> (1)

5. <u>make</u> (1)

6. <u>shape</u> (1)

Read directions to children.
Spelling
© Houghton Mifflin Harcourt Publishing Company. All rights reserved.
183
Assessment Tip: Total 6 points
Grade 1, Unit 3: Nature Near and Far

Verbs with *ed*

✏️ Circle the verbs that tell about the past. Write those verbs.

1. The game <u>started</u> at one.
   starts (started) (2 points)

2. Stan <u>filled</u> the box.
   fills (filled) (2)

3. Jane <u>looked</u> at the pictures.
   looks (looked) (2)

4. The frog <u>jumped</u> very far.
   jumps (jumped) (2)

5. Mr. Scott <u>picked</u> the best one.
   picks (picked) (2)

Read directions to children.
Grammar
© Houghton Mifflin Harcourt Publishing Company. All rights reserved.
184
Assessment Tip: Total 10 points
Grade 1, Unit 3: Nature Near and Far

Taking Notes

Listen to this passage about camels. Read along.

Many camels live in deserts. Camels have long legs and humps on their backs. Camels can live to be 50 or even 60 years old. Camels eat plants that grow in the desert.

✏️ Take notes about camels. Use words and pictures. Put your notes in the correct boxes. Sample answers:

Bodies
long legs (1 point)
humps (1)

How Long They Live
50 to 60 years (1)

Food
plants (1)

Read directions and passage to children.
Writing
© Houghton Mifflin Harcourt Publishing Company. All rights reserved.
185
Assessment Tip: Total 4 points
Grade 1, Unit 3: Nature Near and Far

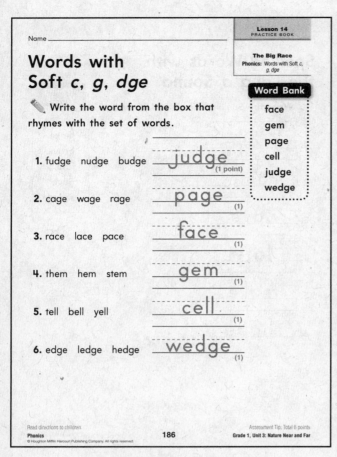

Words with Soft *c, g, dge*

✏️ Write the word from the box that rhymes with the set of words.

Word Bank
face
gem
page
cell
judge
wedge

1. fudge nudge budge   _judge_ (1 point)

2. cage wage rage   _page_ (1)

3. race lace pace   _face_ (1)

4. them hem stem   _gem_ (1)

5. tell bell yell   _cell_ (1)

6. edge ledge hedge   _wedge_ (1)

Read directions to children.
Phonics
© Houghton Mifflin Harcourt Publishing Company. All rights reserved.
186
Assessment Tip: Total 6 points
Grade 1, Unit 3: Nature Near and Far

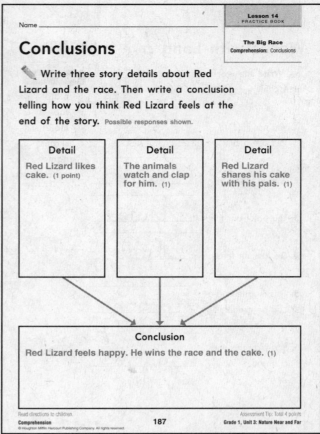

Conclusions

✏️ Write three story details about Red Lizard and the race. Then write a conclusion telling how you think Red Lizard feels at the end of the story. Possible responses shown.

Detail	Detail	Detail
Red Lizard likes cake. (1 point)	The animals watch and clap for him. (1)	Red Lizard shares his cake with his pals. (1)

Conclusion
Red Lizard feels happy. He wins the race and the cake. (1)

Read directions to children.
Comprehension
© Houghton Mifflin Harcourt Publishing Company. All rights reserved.
187
Assessment Tip: Total 4 points
Grade 1, Unit 3: Nature Near and Far

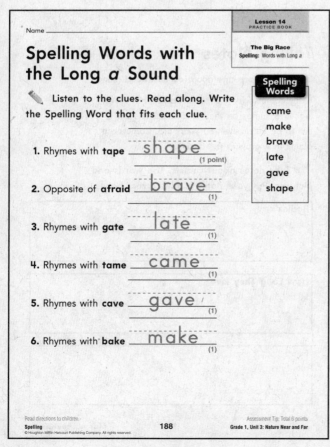

Spelling Words with the Long *a* Sound

✏️ Listen to the clues. Read along. Write the Spelling Word that fits each clue.

Spelling Words
came
make
brave
late
gave
shape

1. Rhymes with **tape** _shape_ (1 point)

2. Opposite of **afraid** _brave_ (1)

3. Rhymes with **gate** _late_ (1)

4. Rhymes with **tame** _came_ (1)

5. Rhymes with **cave** _gave_ (1)

6. Rhymes with **bake** _make_ (1)

Read directions to children.
Spelling
© Houghton Mifflin Harcourt Publishing Company. All rights reserved.
188
Assessment Tip: Total 6 points
Grade 1, Unit 3: Nature Near and Far

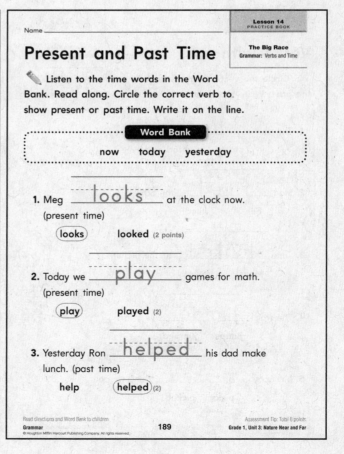

Present and Past Time

✏️ Listen to the time words in the Word Bank. Read along. Circle the correct verb to show present or past time. Write it on the line.

Word Bank
now   today   yesterday

1. Meg _looks_ at the clock now.
(present time)
   (looks)   looked (2 points)

2. Today we _play_ games for math.
(present time)
   (play)   played (2)

3. Yesterday Ron _helped_ his dad make lunch. (past time)
   help   (helped) (2)

Read directions and Word Bank to children.
Grammar
© Houghton Mifflin Harcourt Publishing Company. All rights reserved.
189
Assessment Tip: Total 6 points
Grade 1, Unit 3: Nature Near and Far

Spelling Words with the Long *a* Sound

✏️ Write a Spelling Word from the box to complete each sentence.

Spelling Words

came
late
make
brave
shape
gave

1. I got here ___late___ (1 point)

2. Will you ___make___ me a cake? (1)

3. He ___came___ to play with me. (1)

4. Max is big and ___brave___ . (1)

5. He ___gave___ me a new pen. (1)

6. What ___shape___ is that box? (1)

Read directions to children.
Spelling
© Houghton Mifflin Harcourt Publishing Company. All rights reserved.
190
Assessment Tip: Total 6 points
Grade 1, Unit 3: Nature Near and Far

Spiral Review

✏️ Listen to the nouns. Read along. Circle the correct noun to name each picture. Then write the noun.

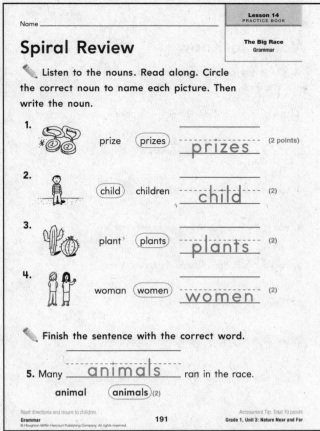

1. prize (prizes) ___prizes___ (2 points)

2. (child) children ___child___ (2)

3. plant (plants) ___plants___ (2)

4. woman (women) ___women___ (2)

✏️ Finish the sentence with the correct word.

5. Many ___animals___ ran in the race.

   animal (animals) (2)

Read directions and nouns to children.
Grammar
© Houghton Mifflin Harcourt Publishing Company. All rights reserved.
191
Assessment Tip: Total 10 points
Grade 1, Unit 3: Nature Near and Far

Planning My Report

✏️ Write a question about the animal you choose. Then find and write facts to answer your question. Responses will vary.

My Topic: (1 point) _____

My Question (1)

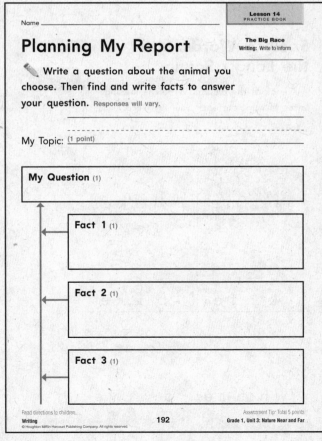

Fact 1 (1)

Fact 2 (1)

Fact 3 (1)

Read directions to children.
Writing
© Houghton Mifflin Harcourt Publishing Company. All rights reserved.
192
Assessment Tip: Total 5 points
Grade 1, Unit 3: Nature Near and Far

Grammar in Writing

• Some verbs tell what is happening now. Some verbs tell what happened in the past.
• Add **ed** to most verbs to tell about the past.

✏️ Listen to the time words in the Word Bank. Read along. Fix the mistakes in these sentences. Use proofreading marks.

Word Bank

now   yesterday   last night

Example: Many people ~~watch~~ the race last night.
                                    watched

1. The animals played now. (2 points)
                      play

2. The frog and snake talk yesterday. (2)
                          talked

3. Last night the rat visits the duck. (2)
                       visited

Proofreading Marks	
∧	add
⤶	take out

Read directions to children.
Grammar
© Houghton Mifflin Harcourt Publishing Company. All rights reserved.
193
Assessment Tip: Total 6 points
Grade 1, Unit 3: Nature Near and Far

Words to Know

✏️ Circle the correct word to complete each sentence.

1. Lan goes for a (**walk,** bird) in the park. (1 point)

2. It is a very (both, **long**) path. (1)

3. Lan sees a (or, **bird**) in its nest. (1)

4. Will it (**fly,** long) away when it sees her? (1)

5. Two ducks in the lake are (bird, **both**) wet. (1)

6. Their (**eyes,** walk) are black. (1)

7. Lan likes to watch (**those,** eyes) ducks. (1)

8. Lan has to go now (fly, **or**) she will be late. (1)

Words with Long *i*

✏️ Circle the word that matches the picture.

1. bake (**bike**) (1 point)

2. (**dime**) dim (1)

3. print (**prize**) (1)

4. pale (**pipe**) (1)

5. miss (**mice**) (1)

6. (**hive**) have (1)

Words with Long *i*

✏️ Write the word that best completes each sentence. Use words from the Word Bank.

Word Bank
- time
- smile
- ride
- like
- kite

1. Pat and I ____like____ to play. (1 point)

2. Pat likes to ____ride____ her bike. (1)

3. I like to fly my ____kite____. (1)

4. Pat is fun. She makes me ____smile____. (1)

5. We have a good ____time____. (1)

Spelling Words with the Long *i* Sound

✏️ Look at the picture. Write the missing letter to complete each Spelling Word.

Spelling Words
- drive
- time
- bike
- white
- kite
- like

1. t **i** m e (1 point)

2. l **i** k e (1)

3. k **i** t e (1)

4. b **i** k e (1)

5. w h **i** t e (1)

6. d r **i** v e (1)

Using *is* and *are*

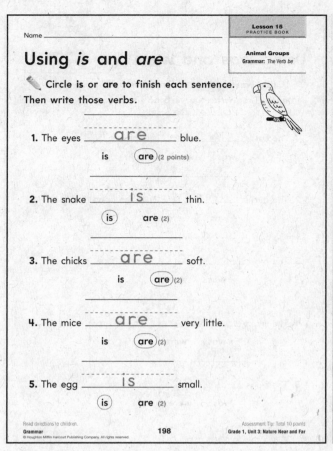

✏️ Circle **is** or **are** to finish each sentence. Then write those verbs.

1. The eyes ___are___ blue.

   is   (are) (2 points)

2. The snake ___is___ thin.

   (is)   are (2)

3. The chicks ___are___ soft.

   is   (are) (2)

4. The mice ___are___ very little.

   is   (are) (2)

5. The egg ___is___ small.

   (is)   are (2)

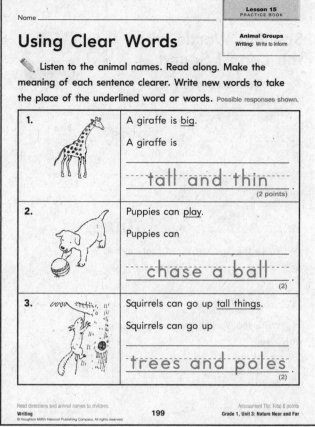

Using Clear Words

✏️ Listen to the animal names. Read along. Make the meaning of each sentence clearer. Write new words to take the place of the underlined word or words. Possible responses shown.

1.	A giraffe is <u>big</u>. A giraffe is ___tall and thin___ (2 points)
2.	Puppies can <u>play</u>. Puppies can ___chase a ball___ (2)
3.	Squirrels can go up <u>tall things</u>. Squirrels can go up ___trees and poles___ (2)

Digraphs *kn, wr, gn, mb*

✏️ Circle the two words in each row that begin or end with the same sound. Write the letters that spell the sound.

| kn | wr | gn | mb |

1.	(wrap) white (wrist) (1 point)	w r
2.	(lamb) (numb) crab (1)	m b
3.	kite (knot) (knack) (1)	k n
4.	grape (gnash) (gnat) (1)	g n
5.	(write) water (wren) (1)	w r
6.	(knife) (knit) kick (1)	k n

Compare and Contrast

✏️ Write things about birds in the first oval. Write things about mammals in the other oval. Then write things about both of them where the ovals connect. Possible responses shown.

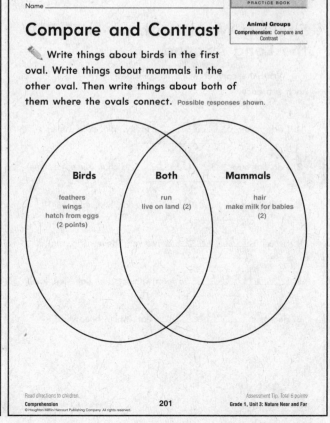

Birds
feathers
wings
hatch from eggs
(2 points)

Both
run
live on land (2)

Mammals
hair
make milk for babies
(2)

Spelling Words with the Long *i* Sound

✎ Write the Spelling Words that rhyme with **hike**.

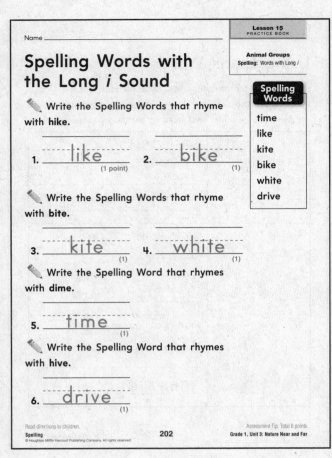

Spelling Words

time
like
kite
bike
white
drive

1. like
(1 point)

2. bike
(1)

✎ Write the Spelling Words that rhyme with **bite**.

3. kite
(1)

4. white
(1)

✎ Write the Spelling Word that rhymes with **dime**.

5. time
(1)

✎ Write the Spelling Word that rhymes with **hive**.

6. drive
(1)

Read directions to children.
Spelling
© Houghton Mifflin Harcourt Publishing Company. All rights reserved.

202

Assessment Tip: Total 6 points
Grade 1, Unit 3: Nature Near and Far

Using *was* and *were*

✎ Circle **was** or **were** to finish each sentence. Then write the verb on the line.

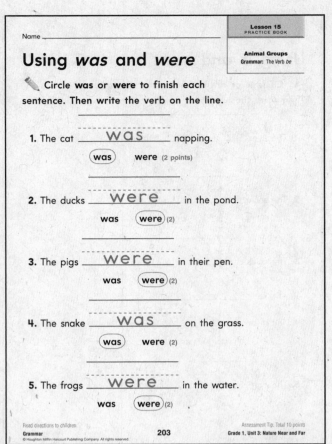

1. The cat ___was___ napping.

(was)   were (2 points)

2. The ducks ___were___ in the pond.

was   (were) (2)

3. The pigs ___were___ in their pen.

was   (were) (2)

4. The snake ___was___ on the grass.

(was)   were (2)

5. The frogs ___were___ in the water.

was   (were) (2)

Read directions to children.
Grammar
© Houghton Mifflin Harcourt Publishing Company. All rights reserved.

203

Assessment Tip: Total 10 points
Grade 1, Unit 3: Nature Near and Far

Spelling Words with the Long *i* Sound

✎ Write the correct word to complete each sentence.

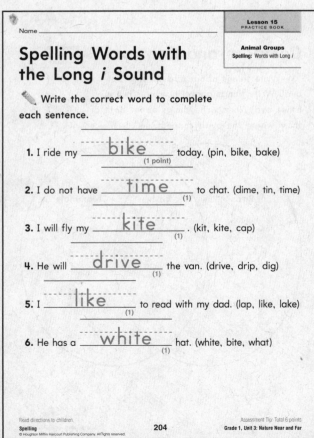

1. I ride my ___bike___ today. (pin, bike, bake)
(1 point)

2. I do not have ___time___ to chat. (dime, tin, time)
(1)

3. I will fly my ___kite___. (kit, kite, cap)
(1)

4. He will ___drive___ the van. (drive, drip, dig)
(1)

5. I ___like___ to read with my dad. (lap, like, lake)
(1)

6. He has a ___white___ hat. (white, bite, what)
(1)

Read directions to children.
Spelling
© Houghton Mifflin Harcourt Publishing Company. All rights reserved.

204

Assessment Tip: Total 6 points
Grade 1, Unit 3: Nature Near and Far

Spiral Review

✎ Circle the preposition in each sentence. Decide if the preposition tells where or when. Write **where** or **when** on the line.

1. Fish swim (in) the lake.   ___where___
(1 point)

2. The pup drinks (after) its mom has a drink.   ___when___
(1)

3. The frog sits (on) a rock.   ___where___
(1)

4. The fox runs (up) a hill.   ___where___
(1)

5. The dog wakes (at) five.   ___when___
(1)

6. Ducks fly (over) the pond.   ___where___
(1)

Read directions to children.
Grammar
© Houghton Mifflin Harcourt Publishing Company. All rights reserved.

205

Assessment Tip: Total 6 points
Grade 1, Unit 3: Nature Near and Far

Grammar in Writing

- The verbs **is** and **are** tell what is happening now. The verbs **was** and **were** tell what happened in the past.
- Use **is** or **was** with a noun that names one.

✎ **Fix the mistakes in these sentences. Use proofreading marks.**

     Example: Frogs ~~was~~ once tadpoles. A frog ~~are~~ small.
                  ^were
is^

1. Cats ~~is~~ mammals. (2 points)
      ^are

2. Dogs ~~was~~ once pups. (2)
       ^were

3. The fox ~~were~~ once a cub. (2)
         ^was

4. Apes ~~is~~ strong. (2)
      ^are

Proofreading Marks	
∧	add
⟿	take out

Read directions to children.
Grammar
© Houghton Mifflin Harcourt Publishing Company. All rights reserved.
206
Assessment Tip: Total 8 points
Grade 1, Unit 3: Nature Near and Far

Contents

Name _____

Lesson 16
PRACTICE BOOK

Let's Go to the Moon!
High-Frequency Words

Words to Know

✎ Listen to the clues and read along.
Circle the best answer to each clue.

1. This means **in a circle**.   (around)   think
                                                    (1 point)

2. This means **not heavy**.   because   (light)
                                                    (1)

3. You do this to let people look
   at something.   bring   (show)
                                                    (1)

4. **After** is its opposite.   (before)   carry
                                                    (1)

5. You do this with bags.   (carry)   because
                                                    (1)

6. This tells why.   (because)   around
                                                    (1)

7. **Take away** is its opposite.   light   (bring)
                                                    (1)

8. Your brain does this.   (think)   before
                                                    (1)

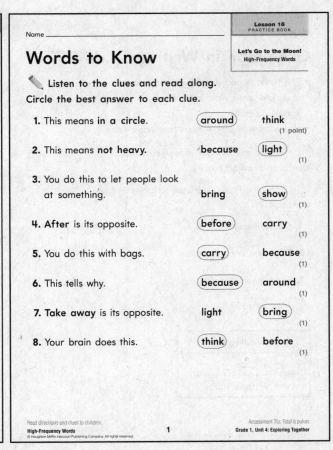

Read directions and clues to children.
High-Frequency Words
© Houghton Mifflin Harcourt Publishing Company. All rights reserved.

Assessment Tip: Total 8 points

1

Grade 1, Unit 4: Exploring Together

Name _____

Lesson 16
PRACTICE BOOK

Let's Go to the Moon!
Phonics: Words with Long o

Words with Long o

✎ Read the word. Circle the picture that
matches the word.

1. home
   (1 point)

2. go
   (1)

3. stone
   (1)

4. robe
   (1)

5. hole
   (1)

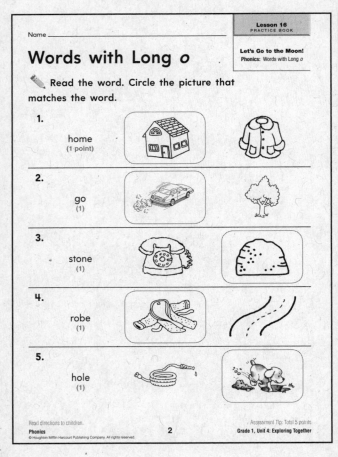

Read directions to children.
Phonics
© Houghton Mifflin Harcourt Publishing Company. All rights reserved.

Assessment Tip: Total 5 points

2

Grade 1, Unit 4: Exploring Together

Name _____

Lesson 16
PRACTICE BOOK

Let's Go to the Moon!
Phonics: Words with Long o

Words with Long o

✎ Look at the picture. Name each picture.
Write the missing letters to complete the word.

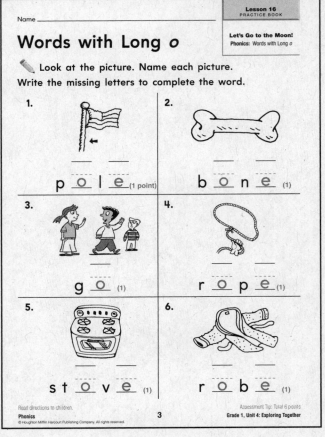

1. p o l e (1 point)   2. b o n e (1)

3. g o (1)   4. r o p e (1)

5. s t o v e (1)   6. r o b e (1)

Read directions to children.
Phonics
© Houghton Mifflin Harcourt Publishing Company. All rights reserved.

Assessment Tip: Total 6 points

3

Grade 1, Unit 4: Exploring Together

Spelling Words with the Long *o* Sound

Lesson 16
PRACTICE BOOK

Let's Go to the Moon!
Spelling: Words with Long *o*

✎ Sort the words. Write the correct Spelling Words in each column.

Spelling Words

so
go
home
hole
no
rope
joke
bone
stove
poke

Ends with **o**	Ends with Silent **e**
so (1 point)	home (1)
go (1)	hole (1)
no (1)	rope (1)
	joke (1)
	bone (1)
	stove (1)
	poke (1)

What Is a Question?

Lesson 16
PRACTICE BOOK

Let's Go to the Moon!
Grammar: Questions

✎ Circle each question.

1. (What did you see?) (1 point)

2. (Can you look up?) (1)

3. (Is that the sun?) (1)

4. I think I will read.

5. (Where did Mike go?) (1)

6. They are at the game.

7. (How many rocks does Liz have?) (1)

8. I like to tell jokes.

Using Details

Lesson 16
PRACTICE BOOK

Let's Go to the Moon!
Writing: Write to Narrate

✎ Draw a picture of something you discovered, or <u>found</u>.

(1 point)

✎ Write sentences about when you <u>saw</u> your discovery.
Responses will vary.

One day I **found** a (1) _____ .

When I **saw** it, I (1) _____ .

Then I (1) _____ .

| Main Idea |

_____

All my sentences tell about (1) _____

Words with Long *u*

Lesson 16
PRACTICE BOOK

Let's Go to the Moon!
Phonics: Words with Long *u*

✎ Circle the word that names the picture.

1.  (flute) flat (1 point)

2. mole (mule) (1)

3. hang (huge) (1)

4. (cute) cut (1)

5. cone (cube) (1)

Main Idea and Details

Let's Go to the Moon!
Comprehension: Main Idea
and Details

Use the web map to show the supporting details about the Moon's surface.

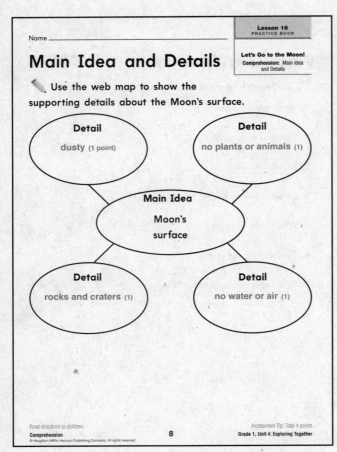

Detail
dusty (1 point)

Detail
no plants or animals (1)

Main Idea
Moon's surface

Detail
rocks and craters (1)

Detail
no water or air (1)

Spelling Words with the Long *o* Sound

Let's Go to the Moon!
Spelling: Words with Long *o*

Write the Spelling Words that rhyme with woke.

1. joke (1 point)   2. poke (1)

Write the Spelling Words that begin with h.

3. home (1)   4. hole (1)

Write the Spelling Words that rhyme with Jo.

5. so (1)

6. go (1)

7. no (1)

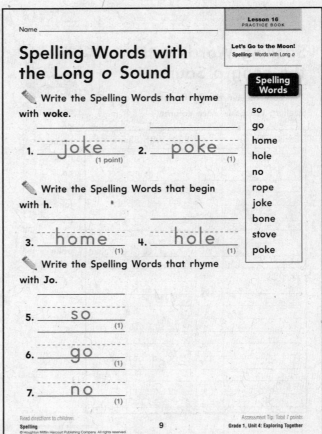

Spelling Words

so
go
home
hole
no
rope
joke
bone
stove
poke

Writing Questions

Let's Go to the Moon!
Grammar: Questions

Write the correct word from the Word Bank to begin each sentence. Write the correct end mark.

Word Bank

What   Can   When   Where   Do   Are

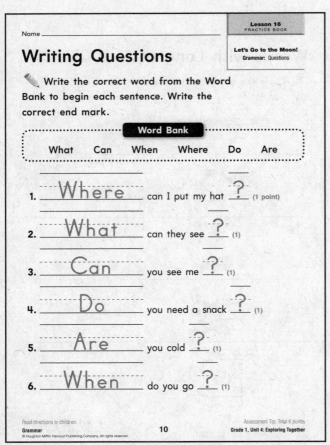

1. Where can I put my hat ? (1 point)

2. What can they see ? (1)

3. Can you see me ? (1)

4. Do you need a snack ? (1)

5. Are you cold ? (1)

6. When do you go ? (1)

Planning My Sentences

Let's Go to the Moon!
Writing: Write to Narrate

Draw and write details that tell what happened. Responses will vary.

My Topic: _____ (1 point)

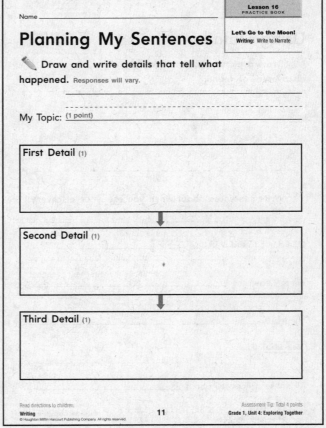

First Detail (1)

Second Detail (1)

Third Detail (1)

Spelling Words with the Long *o* Sound

Lesson 16
PRACTICE BOOK

Let's Go to the Moon!
Spelling: Words with Long *o*

✎ Write a Spelling Word to complete each sentence.

Spelling Words
so
go
home
hole
no
rope
joke
bone
stove
poke

1. The pot on the __stove__ is hot. (1 point)

2. Can you wrap the __rope__ (1) around the pole?

3. What __home__ (1) does a fox live in?

4. I can tell a funny __joke__ (1).

5. Stand up __so__ (1) that I can see you.

6. It is time to __go__ (1) to bed.

Spiral Review

Lesson 16
PRACTICE BOOK

Let's Go to the Moon!
Grammar

✎ Circle each proper noun. Then write the proper noun correctly.

1. My friend (mel) has a box of gem stones. __Mel__ (1 point)

2. She will let (kim) look at it. __Kim__ (1)

3. She has a dog named (red.) __Red__ (1)

✎ Draw a line under each title. Then write the titles and names correctly.

4. Mom's friend is mrs. Dell. __Mrs. Dell__ (1)

5. Will dr. Wade visit the class? __Dr. Wade__ (1)

6. I wrote to mr. Kline. __Mr. Kline__ (1)

Grammar in Writing

Lesson 16
PRACTICE BOOK

Let's Go to the Moon!
Grammar: Questions

A sentence that asks something is called a **question.** A question begins with a capital letter and ends with a **question mark.**

✎ Fix the mistakes in these sentences. Use proofreading marks.

Examples: does the moon have plants?

Is the moon dusty?

1. Did you know his name? (1 point)

2. when did they go? (1)

3. Why do you have your bike? (1)

4. what do cats eat? (1)

5. is the Moon hot or cold? (2)

Proofreading Marks	
∧	Add
≡	Capital letter

Words to Know

Lesson 17
PRACTICE BOOK

The Big Trip
High-Frequency Words

✎ Listen to the questions. Read along. Circle the best answer to each question.

1. What word goes with **might**? (maybe) there (1 point)

2. What word goes with **do not**? car (don't) (1)

3. What word goes with **true**? could (sure) (1)

4. What word goes with **drive**? (car) there (1)

5. What word goes with **here**? (there) don't (1)

6. What word goes with **can**? cart (could) (1)

7. What word comes after the words "This story is _____"? don't (about) (1)

8. What word tells how you travel? (by) maybe (1)

Words with Long *e*

✏️ Circle the word that matches the picture.

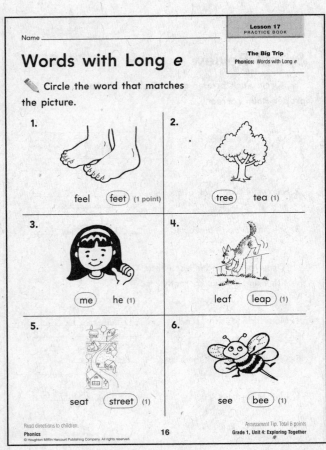

1.
feel (feet) (1 point)

2.
(tree) tea (1)

3.
(me) he (1)

4.
leaf (leap) (1)

5.
seat (street) (1)

6.
see (bee) (1)

Assessment Tip: Total 6 points
Grade 1, Unit 4: Exploring Together

Words with Long *e*

✏️ Circle the word that completes the sentence.

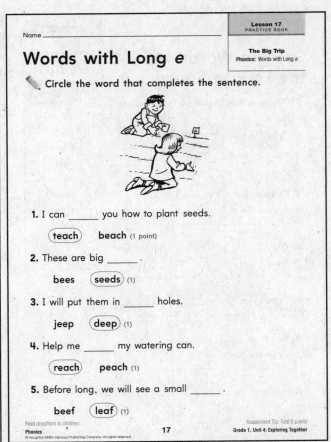

1. I can _____ you how to plant seeds.

(teach)   beach (1 point)

2. These are big _____ .

bees   (seeds) (1)

3. I will put them in _____ holes.

jeep   (deep) (1)

4. Help me _____ my watering can.

(reach)   peach (1)

5. Before long, we will see a small _____ .

beef   (leaf) (1)

Assessment Tip: Total 5 points
Grade 1, Unit 4: Exploring Together

Spelling Words with the Long *e* Sound

✏️ Sort the words. Write the correct Spelling Words in each column.

Spelling Words

me
be
read
feet
tree
keep
eat
mean
sea
these

Words with e	Words with ea	Words with ee
me (1 point)	read (1)	feet (1)
be (1)	eat (1)	tree (1)
	mean (1)	keep (1)
	sea (1)	

Word with Silent e

these (1)

Assessment Tip: Total 10 points
Grade 1, Unit 4: Exploring Together

Question or Statement?

✏️ Draw a line under the correct sentence in each pair.

1. Where are we going.   <u>Where are we going?</u> (1 point)

2. <u>A boat is fun.</u> (1)   A boat is fun?

3. When will we go.   <u>When will we go?</u> (1)

4. Where is your bike.   <u>Where is your bike?</u> (1)

5. <u>Planes are fast.</u> (1)   Planes are fast?

✏️ Write the correct end mark to finish each sentence.

6. Can we go out to play __?__ (1)

7. Tim lost his map __.__ (1)

8. Will your friend come __?__ (1)

Assessment Tip: Total 8 points
Grade 1, Unit 4: Exploring Together

Details for Where and When

✏️ Draw a picture of something you saw or did on a trip.

(1 point)

✏️ Write sentences about your trip.
Responses will vary.

Who	Action	Where
(1)	(1)	(1)

Who	Action	When
(1)	(1)	(1)

Who	Action	Where
(1)	(1)	(1)

Read directions to children.
Writing
© Houghton Mifflin Harcourt Publishing Company. All rights reserved.
20
Assessment Tip: Total 10 points
Grade 1, Unit 4: Exploring Together

Words Ending with *ng, nk*

✏️ Circle the letters that finish the word. Write the word.

1. ba____
(nk, ng)
bank (1 point)

2. dri____
(nk, ng)
drink (1)

3. swi____
(nk, ng)
swing (1)

4. ki____
(nk, ng)
king (1)

Read directions to children.
Phonics
© Houghton Mifflin Harcourt Publishing Company. All rights reserved.
21
Assessment Tip: Total 4 points
Grade 1, Unit 4: Exploring Together

Compare and Contrast

✏️ Use the Venn diagram to tell how Pig's ideas and Goat's ideas are alike and different. Possible responses are shown.

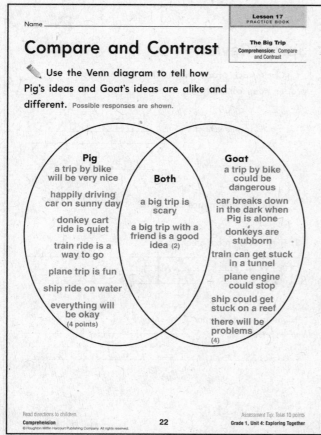

Pig
a trip by bike will be very nice

happily driving car on sunny day

donkey cart ride is quiet

train ride is a way to go

plane trip is fun

ship ride on water

everything will be okay
(4 points)

Both
a big trip is scary

a big trip with a friend is a good idea (2)

Goat
a trip by bike could be dangerous

car breaks down in the dark when Pig is alone

donkeys are stubborn

train can get stuck in a tunnel

plane engine could stop

ship could get stuck on a reef

there will be problems
(4)

Read directions to children.
Comprehension
© Houghton Mifflin Harcourt Publishing Company. All rights reserved.
22
Assessment Tip: Total 10 points
Grade 1, Unit 4: Exploring Together

Spelling Words with the Long *e* Sound

✏️ Write the Spelling Word that names each picture.

Spelling Words
me
be
read
feet
tree
keep
eat
mean
sea
these

1. me (1 point)
2. read (1)
3. feet (1)
4. tree (1)
5. eat (1)
6. sea (1)

Read directions to children.
Spelling
© Houghton Mifflin Harcourt Publishing Company. All rights reserved.
23
Assessment Tip: Total 6 points
Grade 1, Unit 4: Exploring Together

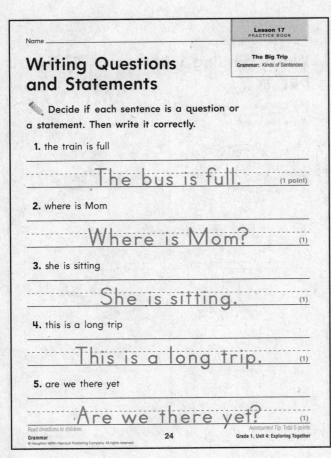

Writing Questions and Statements

✎ Decide if each sentence is a question or a statement. Then write it correctly.

1. the train is full

The bus is full. (1 point)

2. where is Mom

Where is Mom? (1)

3. she is sitting

She is sitting. (1)

4. this is a long trip

This is a long trip. (1)

5. are we there yet

Are we there yet? (1)

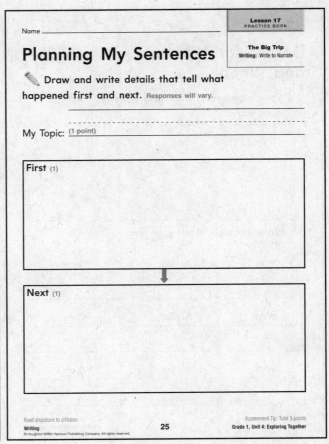

Planning My Sentences

✎ Draw and write details that tell what happened first and next. Responses will vary.

My Topic: (1 point) _____

First (1)

Next (1)

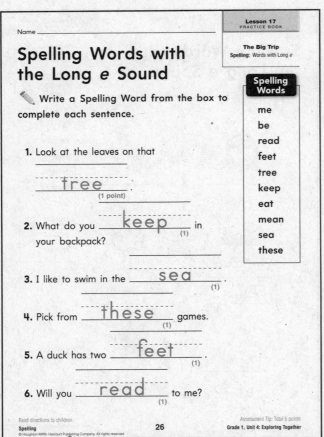

Spelling Words with the Long *e* Sound

✎ Write a Spelling Word from the box to complete each sentence.

Spelling Words

me
be
read
feet
tree
keep
eat
mean
sea
these

1. Look at the leaves on that

tree . (1 point)

2. What do you keep in your backpack? (1)

3. I like to swim in the sea . (1)

4. Pick from these games. (1)

5. A duck has two feet . (1)

6. Will you read to me? (1)

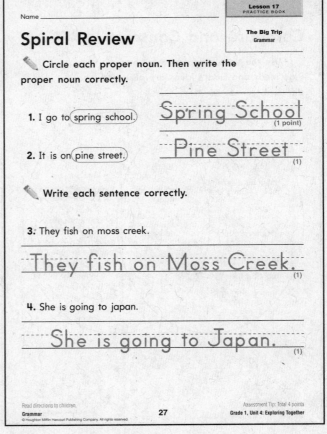

Spiral Review

✎ Circle each proper noun. Then write the proper noun correctly.

1. I go to (spring school.)

Spring School (1 point)

2. It is on (pine street.)

Pine Street (1)

✎ Write each sentence correctly.

3. They fish on moss creek.

They fish on Moss Creek. (1)

4. She is going to japan.

She is going to Japan. (1)

Lesson 17
PRACTICE BOOK

Grammar in Writing

The Big Trip
Grammar: Kinds of Sentences

A **statement** is a telling sentence.

A **question** is an asking sentence.

✎ Write two statements and two questions about the picture. Be sure you begin and end each sentence correctly.

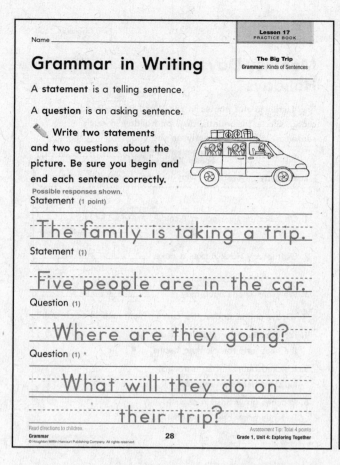

Possible responses shown.

Statement (1 point)

The family is taking a trip.

Statement (1)

Five people are in the car.

Question (1)

Where are they going?

Question (1)

What will they do on their trip?

Lesson 18
PRACTICE BOOK

Words to Know

Where Does Food Come From?
High-Frequency Words

✎ Circle the correct word to complete each sentence.

1. Fran ate her beets (these, (first)). (1 point)

2. Beets are planted in the ((ground), sometimes). (1)

3. (Food, (Sometimes)) Fran eats salad, too. (1)

4. Fran has to eat all the ((food), your) on her plate. (1)

5. "Eat (ground, (your)) peas," said Mom. (1)

6. The peas are (your, (right)) from the shop. (1)

7. Fran looked ((under), first) her peas. (1)

8. Fran said, "((These), Under) peas look good!" (1)

Lesson 18
PRACTICE BOOK

Words with *ai, ay*

Where Does Food Come From?
Phonics: Words with *ai, ay*

✎ Read the words. Circle the word that names the picture. Then write the word.

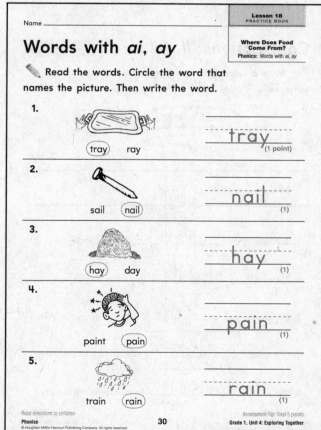

1. (tray) ray — tray (1 point)

2. sail (nail) — nail (1)

3. (hay) day — hay (1)

4. paint (pain) — pain (1)

5. train (rain) — rain (1)

Lesson 18
PRACTICE BOOK

Words with *ai, ay*

Where Does Food Come From?
Phonics: Words with *ai, ay*

✎ Read the words. Circle the word that names the picture.

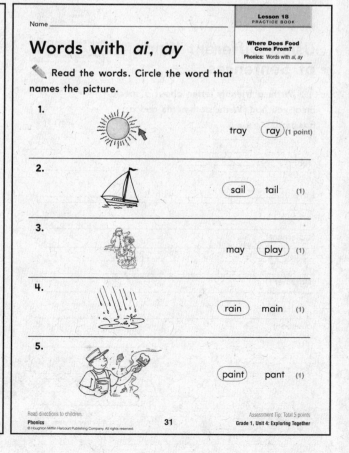

1. tray (ray) (1 point)

2. (sail) tail (1)

3. may (play) (1)

4. (rain) main (1)

5. (paint) pant (1)

Name

Spelling Words with the Vowel Pairs *ai, ay*

✏️ Sort the words. Write the correct Spelling Words in each column.

Spelling Words

play
grain
sail
mail
may
rain
way
day
stay
pain

Words with ai	Words with ay
grain (1 point)	play (1)
sail (1)	may (1)
mail (1)	way (1)
rain (1)	day (1)
pain (1)	stay (1)

Name

Months, Days, and Holidays

✏️ Listen to the names in the Word Bank. Read along. Circle the month, day, or holiday in each sentence. Write it correctly on the line.

Word Bank

Labor Day   Tuesday   May   June   Saturday   August

1. On (labor day) we had a picnic.   Labor Day (1 point)

2. On (tuesday) Hank makes a cake.   Tuesday (1)

3. We plant seeds each (may.)   May (1)

✏️ Draw a line under the correct sentence in each pair.

4. Ike likes June for planting beans. (1)
   Ike likes june for planting beans.

5. I picked beans on Saturday. (1)
   I picked beans on saturday.

6. Peaches grow best in august.
   Peaches grow best in August. (1)

Name

Using Different Kinds of Sentences

✏️ Write a friendly letter about a special meal you had. Write statements and a question. Responses will vary.

Dear (1 point) _____ ,

I ate (1) _____ with (1) _____ .

(1) _____ .
(statement)

(1) _____ .
(statement)

(1) _____ ?
(question)

_____ ,

_____ (1)

Name

Contractions *'ll, 'd*

✏️ Write a word from the box to finish the sentence.

I would   I'd

he'd	she'll	I'd	they'll	we'd

1. Ben said that ___he'd___ be late today. (1 point)

2. Beth said ___she'll___ go to the beach. (1)

3. Mom and Dad said ___they'll___ go out at five. (1)

4. Gus said, "___I'd___ like to play in the sand." (1)

5. We think ___we'd___ like a day at the beach. (1)

Lesson 18
PRACTICE BOOK

Where Does Food
Come From?
Comprehension: Author's
Purpose

Author's Purpose

Use the Inference Map to write details, and then tell the author's purpose.

Detail	Detail	Detail
Tomatoes grow on vines. Tomatoes have to be made into a sauce to make ketchup. (2 points)	Some foods such as potatoes grow under the ground. (2)	Some foods come from animals such as cows. (2)

Purpose

The author wants to tell about where different foods come from. (2)

Lesson 18
PRACTICE BOOK

Where Does Food Come
From?
Spelling: Words with ai, ay

Spelling Words with the Vowel Pairs *ai*, *ay*

Write the Spelling Words that rhyme with **fail**.

1. sail (1 point)   2. mail (1)

Write the Spelling Words that rhyme with **bay**.

3. play (1)   4. may (1)

5. way (1)   6. day (1)

7. stay (1)

Write the Spelling Words that rhyme with **main**.

8. grain (1)   9. rain (1)   10. pain (1)

Spelling Words

play
grain
sail
mail
may
rain
way
day
stay
pain

Lesson 18
PRACTICE BOOK

Where Does Food
Come From?
Grammar: Names of Months,
Days, and Holidays

Commas in Dates

Listen to the names of months in the Word Bank. Read along. Circle the comma in each date.

Word Bank

March   April   May   June   October

1. Ms. Ray moved to the farm on October 25, 2001. (1 point)

2. She planted wheat on March 13, 2002. (1)

3. She got some chicks on May 28, 2004. (1)

4. She had eggs for sale on June 4, 2007. (1)

The date in each sentence is underlined. Write the date correctly.

5. This patch was planted on March 16 2006.

March 16, 2006 (1)

6. The peas were planted on April 23 2007.

April 23, 2007 (1)

Lesson 18
PRACTICE BOOK

Where Does Food Come
From?
Writing: Write to Narrate

Planning My Letter

Write and draw details that tell what happened first, next, and last. Responses will vary.

I will write my letter to (1 point) _____ .

I will tell about (1) _____

First (1)

Next (1)

Last (1)

Name _____

Lesson 18
PRACTICE BOOK

Where Does Food Come From?
Spelling: Words with Long *a*

Spelling Words with the Long *a* Sound

Write the correct word to complete each sentence.

1. Can you come out and __play__? (1 point)

play　　clay

2. In April there is a lot of __rain__. (1)

rake　　rain

3. Let us __sail__ on the lake. (1)

sail　　tail

4. I feel a __pain__ in my leg. (1)

train　　pain

5. Wheat is a __grain__. (1)

grain　　green

Spiral Review

Circle the correct verb. Then write the sentence with the correct verb.

1. The kids (walk, walks) around the pond.

The kids walk around the pond. (1 point)

2. Nine sheep (eat, eats) the grass.

Nine sheep eat the grass. (1)

3. Ducks (flap, flaps) their wings.

Ducks flap their wings. (1)

4. One mule (sleep, sleeps) in the hay.

One mule sleeps in the hay. (1)

5. Pigs (play, plays) in the mud.

Pigs play in the mud. (1)

Name _____

Lesson 18
PRACTICE BOOK

Where Does Food Come From?
Grammar: Names of Months, Days and Holidays

Grammar in Writing

The name of each **month, day,** and **holiday** begins with a capital letter. When you write a date, use a **comma** between the day of the month and the year.

Example:

labor day is monday september 7 2009.

Listen to the names of months and holidays in the Word Bank. Read along. Fix the mistakes in these sentences. Use proofreading marks.

> ### Word Bank
>
> July　　August　　September　　October
>
> December　　New Year's Eve

1. In october it was cold. (1 point)

2. Mr. Potts left on august 22 2004. (1)

3. Every september they sell jam. (1)

4. Ms. Down opened the shop on july 18 2007. (2)

5. new year's eve is on december 31. (4)

Proofreading Marks			
∧	Add	≡	Capital letter

Words to Know

Listen to the clues. Read along. Circle the best answer to each clue.

1. This means **finished.**　　paper　　(done) (1 point)

2. This is in a short while.　　(soon)　　great (1)

3. This means **speak.**　　were　　(talk) (1)

4. **Awful** is its opposite.　　(great)　　soon (1)

5. A joke makes you do this.　　(laugh)　　done (1)

6. You write on this.　　work　　(paper) (1)

7. This is a **job.**　　great　　(work) (1)

8. Past for **are.**　　laugh　　(were) (1)

Words with *oa, ow*

✏️ Read the word. Circle the picture that matches the word.

1. boat
(1 point)

2. crow
(1)

3. goat
(1)

4. bowl
(1)

5. loaf
(1)

Words with *oa, ow*

✏️ Circle the two words in each row that rhyme. Then write the letters that spell the long **o** sound.

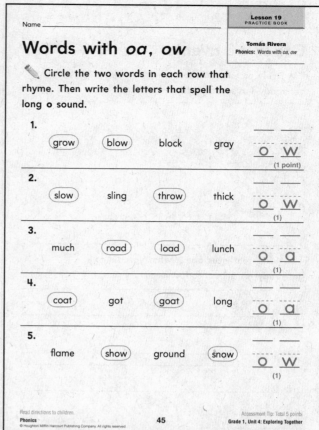

1. (grow) (blow) block gray   o w
(1 point)

2. (slow) sling (throw) thick   o w
(1)

3. much (road) (load) lunch   o a
(1)

4. (coat) got (goat) long   o a
(1)

5. flame (show) ground (snow)   o w
(1)

Spelling Words with Vowel Pairs *oa, ow*

✏️ Sort the words. Write the correct Spelling Words in each column.

Spelling Words
show
row
boat
blow
toad
road
low
coat
grow
snow

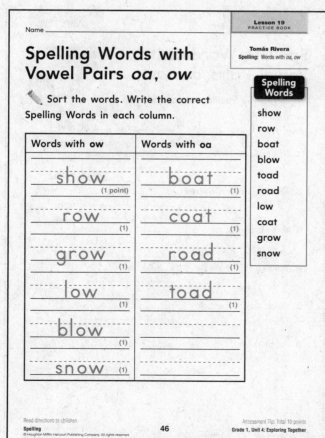

Words with **ow**	Words with **oa**
show (1 point)	boat (1)
row (1)	coat (1)
grow (1)	road (1)
low (1)	toad (1)
blow (1)	
snow (1)	

Future Using *will*

✏️ Circle the sentences that tell about the future. Rewrite the other sentences to tell about the future using *will*.

1. I read each day.

2. (Brent will meet you at the shop.) (1 point)

3. My dad helps me read.

4. They washed the van.

5. (Fran will beat the eggs.) (1)

6. I will read each day. (1)

7. My dad will help me read. (1)

8. They will wash the van. (1)

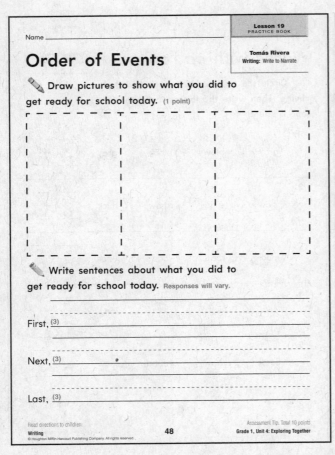

Order of Events

✏️ Draw pictures to show what you did to get ready for school today. (1 point)

✏️ Write sentences about what you did to get ready for school today. Responses will vary.

First, (3)

Next, (3)

Last, (3)

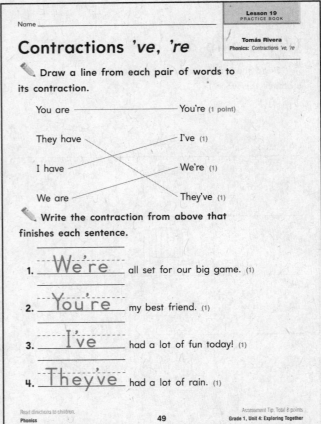

Contractions 've, 're

✏️ Draw a line from each pair of words to its contraction.

You are ——————— You're (1 point)

They have ——————— I've (1)

I have ——————— We're (1)

We are ——————— They've (1)

✏️ Write the contraction from above that finishes each sentence.

1. We're all set for our big game. (1)

2. You're my best friend. (1)

3. I've had a lot of fun today! (1)

4. They've had a lot of rain. (1)

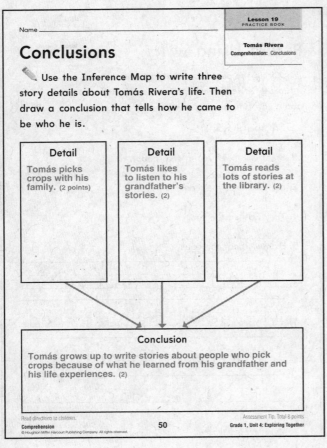

Conclusions

✏️ Use the Inference Map to write three story details about Tomás Rivera's life. Then draw a conclusion that tells how he came to be who he is.

Detail	Detail	Detail
Tomás picks crops with his family. (2 points)	Tomás likes to listen to his grandfather's stories. (2)	Tomás reads lots of stories at the library. (2)

Conclusion

Tomás grows up to write stories about people who pick crops because of what he learned from his grandfather and his life experiences. (2)

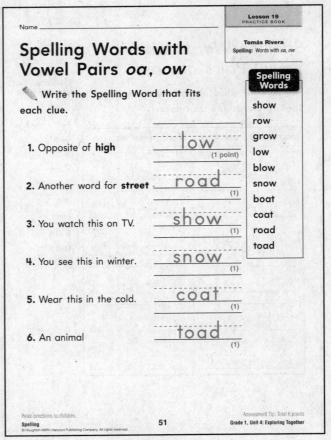

Spelling Words with Vowel Pairs oa, ow

✏️ Write the Spelling Word that fits each clue.

Spelling Words
show
row
grow
low
blow
snow
boat
coat
road
toad

1. Opposite of **high** — low (1 point)

2. Another word for **street** — road (1)

3. You watch this on TV. — show (1)

4. You see this in winter. — snow (1)

5. Wear this in the cold. — coat (1)

6. An animal — toad (1)

Name _____

Future Using *going to*

Tomás Rivera
Grammar: Future Tense

🖊 Circle the sentences that tell about the future. Rewrite the other sentences to tell about the future. Use **going to** in each one.

1. I work with Ed.

2. (Ed is going to have many crops.) (1 point)

3. My dad planted beets.

4. They pulled the weeds.

5. (Jen is going to pick beans with Sam.) (1)

6. Tess has a pet cat.

7. _____ I am going to work with Ed. _____ (1)

8. _____ My dad is going to plant beets. _____ (1)

9. _____ They are going to pull the weeds. _____ (1)

10. _____ Tess is going to have a pet cat. _____ (1)

Name _____

Spelling Words with the Long *o* Sound

Tomás Rivera
Spelling: Words with Long *o*

🖊 Write the correct word to complete each sentence.

1. The class will put on a ___ show ___ .
(1 point)
show   snow

2. The ___ toad ___ hopped on the grass.
(1)
toad   load

3. How do plants ___ grow ___ ?
(1)
throw   grow

4. The ___ boat ___ came in with fish.
(1)
boat   bat

5. Which ___ row ___ will you sit in?
(1)
row   read

Name _____

Spiral Review

Tomás Rivera
Grammar

🖊 Notice the clue word **yesterday** that tells about the past. Circle the verb that tells about the past. Then write those verbs.

1. **Yesterday** mom (works, (worked)) at the new shop.

_____ worked _____ (2 points)

2. She (opens, (opened)) the shop at nine.

_____ opened _____ (2)

3. Many kids (walk, (walked)) into the shop.

_____ walked _____ (2)

4. Val (asks, (asked)) for a new game.

_____ asked _____ (2)

5. Her mom (helps, (helped)) her.

_____ helped _____ (2)

Name _____

Planning My Personal Narrative

Tomás Rivera
Writing: Write to Narrate

🖊 Draw and write details that tell what happened first, next, and last. Responses will vary.

My Topic: (1 point) _____

First (1)

↓

Next (1)

↓

Last (1)

Grammar in Writing

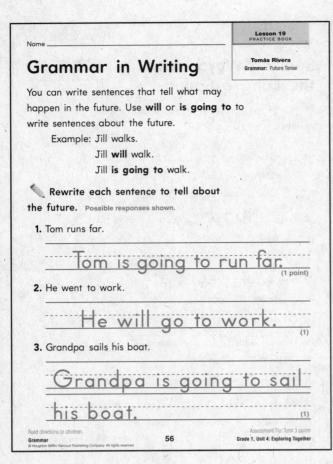

You can write sentences that tell what may happen in the future. Use **will** or **is going to** to write sentences about the future.

Example: Jill walks.

Jill **will** walk.

Jill **is going to** walk.

Rewrite each sentence to tell about the future. **Possible responses shown.**

1. Tom runs far.

Tom is going to run far. (1 point)

2. He went to work.

He will go to work. (1)

3. Grandpa sails his boat.

Grandpa is going to sail his boat. (1)

Assessment Tip: Total 3 points
Grade 1, Unit 4: Exploring Together

Words to Know

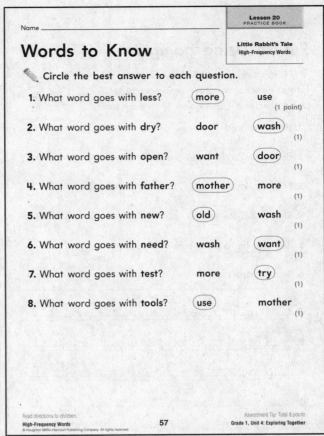

Circle the best answer to each question.

1. What word goes with **less**?   (more)   use
(1 point)

2. What word goes with **dry**?   door   (wash)
(1)

3. What word goes with **open**?   want   (door)
(1)

4. What word goes with **father**?   (mother)   more
(1)

5. What word goes with **new**?   (old)   wash
(1)

6. What word goes with **need**?   wash   (want)
(1)

7. What word goes with **test**?   more   (try)
(1)

8. What word goes with **tools**?   (use)   mother
(1)

Assessment Tip: Total 8 points
Grade 1, Unit 4: Exploring Together

Compound Words

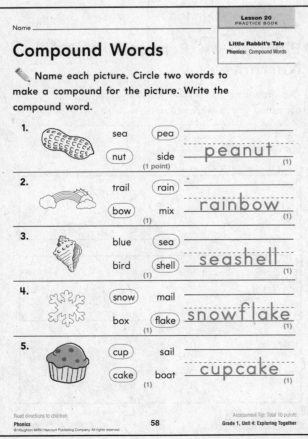

Name each picture. Circle two words to make a compound for the picture. Write the compound word.

1. sea   (pea)
(nut)   side   **peanut** (1)
(1 point)

2. trail   (rain)
(bow)   mix   **rainbow** (1)
(1)

3. blue   (sea)
bird   (shell)   **seashell** (1)
(1)

4. (snow)   mail
box   (flake)   **snowflake** (1)
(1)

5. (cup)   sail
(cake)   boat   **cupcake** (1)
(1)

Assessment Tip: Total 10 points
Grade 1, Unit 4: Exploring Together

Compound Words

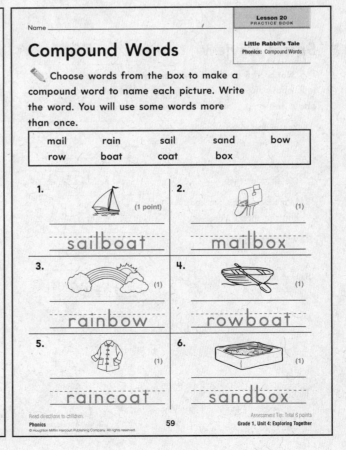

Choose words from the box to make a compound word to name each picture. Write the word. You will use some words more than once.

mail	rain	sail	sand	bow
row	boat	coat	box	

1. **sailboat** (1 point)

2. **mailbox** (1 point)

3. **rainbow** (1)

4. **rowboat** (1)

5. **raincoat** (1)

6. **sandbox** (1)

Assessment Tip: Total 6 points
Grade 1, Unit 4: Exploring Together

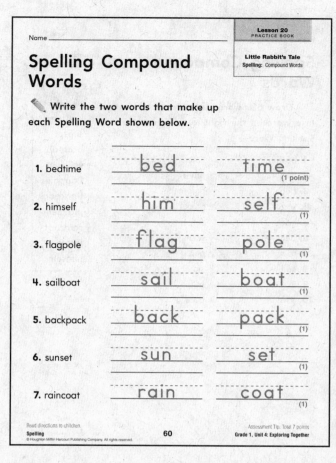

Spelling Compound Words

✏️ Write the two words that make up each Spelling Word shown below.

1. bedtime   bed   time (1 point)
2. himself   him   self (1)
3. flagpole   flag   pole (1)
4. sailboat   sail   boat (1)
5. backpack   back   pack (1)
6. sunset   sun   set (1)
7. raincoat   rain   coat (1)

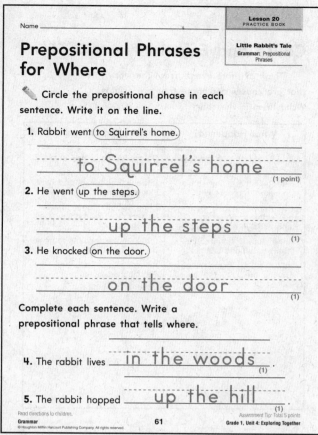

Prepositional Phrases for Where

✏️ Circle the prepositional phase in each sentence. Write it on the line.

1. Rabbit went (to Squirrel's home.)

to Squirrel's home (1 point)

2. He went (up the steps.)

up the steps (1)

3. He knocked (on the door.)

on the door (1)

Complete each sentence. Write a prepositional phrase that tells where.

4. The rabbit lives in the woods . (1)

5. The rabbit hopped up the hill . (1)

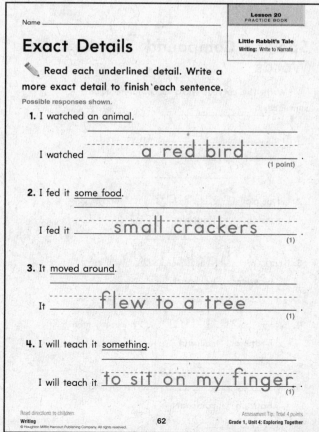

Exact Details

✏️ Read each underlined detail. Write a more exact detail to finish each sentence.

Possible responses shown.

1. I watched an animal.

I watched a red bird (1 point)

2. I fed it some food.

I fed it small crackers (1)

3. It moved around.

It flew to a tree (1)

4. I will teach it something.

I will teach it to sit on my finger (1)

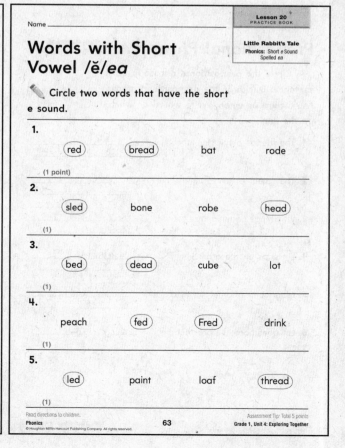

Words with Short Vowel /ĕ/ea

✏️ Circle two words that have the short e sound.

1. (red) (bread) bat rode (1 point)

2. (sled) bone robe (head) (1)

3. (bed) (dead) cube lot (1)

4. peach (fed) (Fred) drink (1)

5. (led) paint loaf (thread) (1)

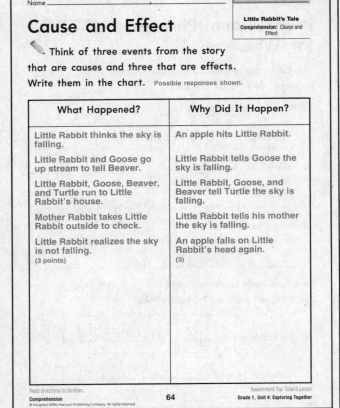

Cause and Effect

✏ Think of three events from the story that are causes and three that are effects. Write them in the chart. **Possible responses shown.**

What Happened?	Why Did It Happen?
Little Rabbit thinks the sky is falling.	An apple hits Little Rabbit.
Little Rabbit and Goose go up stream to tell Beaver.	Little Rabbit tells Goose the sky is falling.
Little Rabbit, Goose, Beaver, and Turtle run to Little Rabbit's house.	Little Rabbit, Goose, and Beaver tell Turtle the sky is falling.
Mother Rabbit takes Little Rabbit outside to check.	Little Rabbit tells his mother the sky is falling.
Little Rabbit realizes the sky is not falling. (3 points)	An apple falls on Little Rabbit's head again. (3)

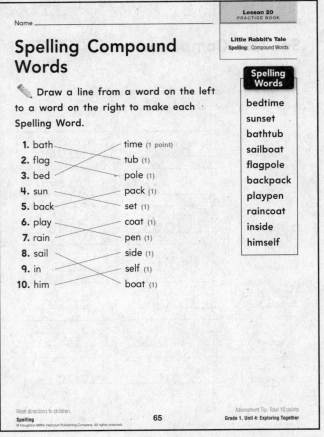

Spelling Compound Words

✏ Draw a line from a word on the left to a word on the right to make each Spelling Word.

1. bath — time (1 point)
2. flag — tub (1)
3. bed — pole (1)
4. sun — pack (1)
5. back — set (1)
6. play — coat (1)
7. rain — pen (1)
8. sail — side (1)
9. in — self (1)
10. him — boat (1)

Spelling Words

bedtime
sunset
bathtub
sailboat
flagpole
backpack
playpen
raincoat
inside
himself

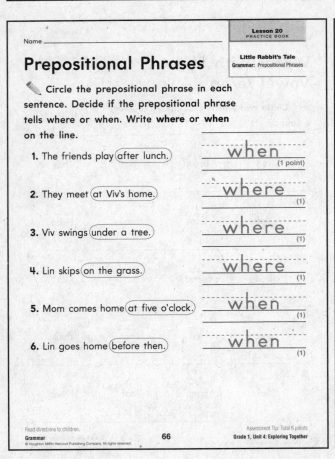

Prepositional Phrases

✏ Circle the prepositional phrase in each sentence. Decide if the prepositional phrase tells where or when. Write **where** or **when** on the line.

1. The friends play (after lunch.) — when (1 point)

2. They meet (at Viv's home.) — where (1)

3. Viv swings (under a tree.) — where (1)

4. Lin skips (on the grass.) — where (1)

5. Mom comes home (at five o'clock.) — when (1)

6. Lin goes home (before then.) — when (1)

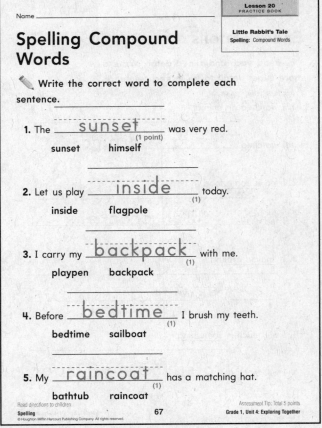

Spelling Compound Words

✏ Write the correct word to complete each sentence.

1. The ___sunset___ was very red. (1 point)
   sunset   himself

2. Let us play ___inside___ today. (1)
   inside   flagpole

3. I carry my ___backpack___ with me. (1)
   playpen   backpack

4. Before ___bedtime___ I brush my teeth. (1)
   bedtime   sailboat

5. My ___raincoat___ has a matching hat. (1)
   bathtub   raincoat

Spiral Review

✎ Write each sentence with the correct verb.

1. This puppet (is, are) small.

This puppet is small.
(1 point)

2. Raindrops (is, are) wet.

Raindrops are wet.
(1)

3. The lambs (is, are) white.

The lambs are white.
(1)

4. The show (was, were) funny.

The show was funny.
(1)

5. Those muffins (was, were) huge.

Those muffins were huge.
(1)

Name _____

Lesson 20
PRACTICE BOOK

Little Rabbit's Tale
Grammar: Prepositional
Phrases

Grammar in Writing

A prepositional phrase can tell when or where.

Example: We walk **after lunch**.   when
We walk **in the park**.   where

✎ Add a prepositional phrase to each sentence to tell when or where. Write the new sentence on the line.

Possible responses shown.

1. My friends and I ran.
(1 point)

My friends and I ran around the track.

2. Something fell.
(1)

Something fell on my head.

3. I tripped.
(1)

I tripped on the stairs.

4. I went home.
(1)

I went home after lunch.

Words to Know

✎ Circle the correct word to complete each sentence.

1. Ben (night, (saw)) the new slide today. (1 point)

2. This swing is ((better,) saw) than that swing. (1)

3. The green leaves ((turned,) told) yellow and red. (1)

4. Nan (window, (thought)) about what to bake. (1)

5. Dad's car is getting (saw, (pretty)) old. (1)

6. Some animals hunt at ((night,) pretty). (1)

7. Close your (better, (window)) when it rains. (1)

8. Jen ((told,) thought) us about her trip. (1)

Words with *ar*

✎ Circle the word that matches the picture.

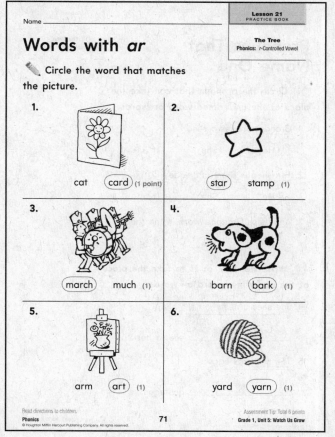

1. cat (card) (1 point)

2. (star) stamp (1)

3. (march) much (1)

4. barn (bark) (1)

5. arm (art) (1)

6. yard (yarn) (1)

Words with *ar*

✏️ Look at the picture and read the words.
Write the word that matches the picture.

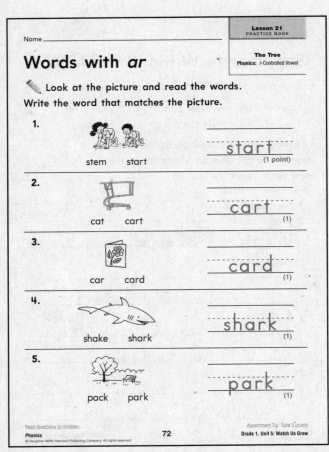

1. stem   start   **start** (1 point)

2. cat   cart   **cart** (1)

3. car   card   **card** (1)

4. shake   shark   **shark** (1)

5. pack   park   **park** (1)

Spelling Words with *r*-Controlled Vowel *ar*

Spelling Words

far
arm
yard
art
jar
bar
barn
bark
card
yarn

✏️ Write the Spelling Words that rhyme
with **far**, **yard**, and **barn**.

1. **Far** rhymes with **jar** (1 point)

and **bar** (1).

2. **Yard** rhymes with **card** (1).

3. **Barn** rhymes with **yarn** (1).

✏️ Write the Spelling Word that names
the picture.

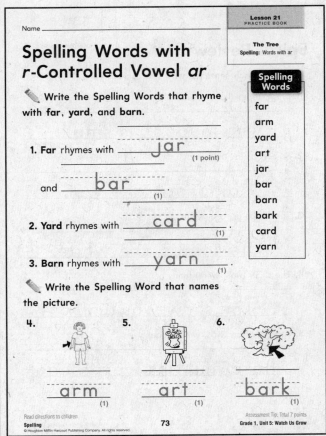

4. **arm** (1)   5. **art** (1)   6. **bark** (1)

Pronouns That Name One

✏️ Circle the pronoun that can take the
place of the underlined word or words.

1. Grandpa makes a shed.

   (He)   She   It (1 point)

2. The shed is short and wide.

   He   She   (It) (1)

3. Ann helps Grandpa work in the shed.

   He   (She)   It (1)

✏️ Write **He**, **She**, or **It** to take the place
of the underlined word or words.

4. Joe sees a nest.

   He sees a nest. (1)

5. The nest has eggs.

   It has eggs. (1)

Dialogue

✏️ Name another animal that Poppleton
could have asked about his tree. Then write
what the two characters might have said.

Responses will vary.

Poppleton still did not know what to do with his tree.

_____

He asked (1 point) _____ what to do.

"_____
(2) _____

_____ ?" Poppleton

asked.

"_____
(2) _____

_____ ," said his friend.

Words with or, ore

🖊 Read the sentences. Circle the sentence that tells about the picture.

1. (We look at the score.) (1 point)

   We look at the star.

2. I like to do chores.

   (I snore when I sleep.) (1)

3. (She finds shells at the shore.) (1)

   She finds fish at the shop.

4. He can play the thorn.

   (He can play the horn.) (1)

5. Here is a jar.

   (Here is a fork.) (1)

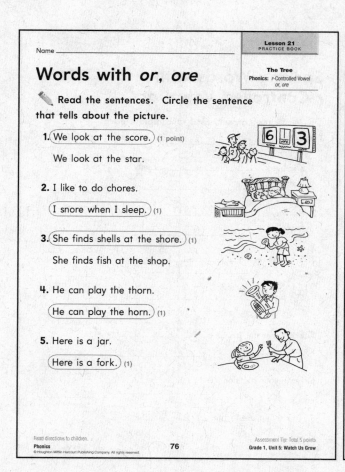

Story Structure

🖊 Write or draw pictures to show the characters, setting, and plot of the story.

Characters	Setting
Poppleton, the tree doctor, Hudson, Newhouse, Cherry Sue, the birds (3 points)	Poppleton's yard (1)

Plot

Beginning

Poppleton planted a tree. The tree got sick. (2)

Middle

People tried to help fix the tree. (2)

End

Cherry Sue told Poppleton to get a bird feeder.

Birds came to visit and the tree got well. (2)

Spelling Words with r-Controlled Vowel ar

🖊 Write the Spelling Word that names the picture.

Spelling Words

far
arm
yard
art
jar
bar
barn
bark
card
yarn

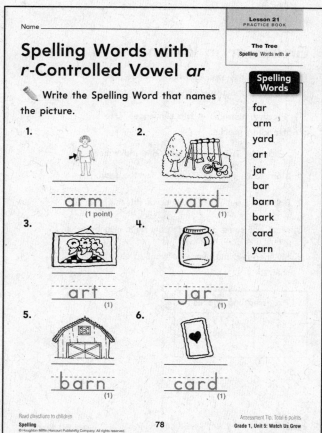

1. arm (1 point)

2. yard (1)

3. art (1)

4. jar (1)

5. barn (1)

6. card (1)

Pronouns That Name More Than One

🖊 Circle the pronoun that can take the place of each underlined subject.

1. <u>Workers</u> plant trees in the park.

   We   (They) (1 point)

2. <u>The trees</u> grow big.

   We   (They) (1)

3. <u>Sis and I</u> sit under the trees.

   (We)   They (1)

🖊 Write **We** or **They** to take the place of each underlined subject.

4. <u>Dad and I</u> walk to the park.

   _____We_____ walk to the park. (1)

5. <u>Pete and Kate</u> run and play.

   _____They_____ run and play. (1)

Planning My Sentences

✏️ Write and draw details that tell what happened **first** and **next**. Responses will vary.

Topic: After Poppleton and Cherry Sue watched the

_____

birds, they (2 points) _____ .

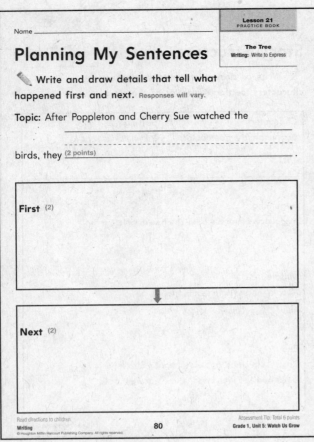

First (2)

Next (2)

Spelling Words with *r*-Controlled Vowel *ar*

✏️ Write the correct word to complete each sentence.

1. She lives ____far____ away from me. (1 point)
fun far

2. He waves his ____arm____ in the air. (1)
ants arm

3. We play in the ____yard____ (1)
yard yarn

4. We paint in ____art____ class. (1)
art part

5. She gave me a ____jar____ of jam. (1)
bar jar

6. Hang your coats on the ____bar____ (1)
card bar

7. The sheep are in the ____barn____ . (1)
barn big

Spiral Review

✏️ Draw a line under each question.

1. What sort of tree is this? (1 point)

2. Do all trees have leaves? (1)

3. Pine trees have cones.

4. What animals live in trees? (1)

5. Birds live in trees.

6. Do we need trees? (1)

7. Trees give us air.

8. Do we get food from trees? (1)

Grammar in Writing

The pronouns **he, she,** and **it** name one. The pronouns **we** and **they** name more than one.

✏️ Fix the mistakes in the sentences. Use proofreading marks.

Example: The shed is done. ~~She~~ It looks nice.

1. Mom saws. ~~He~~ She makes a shelf for the shed. (1 point)

2. Bob and I get paint. ~~They~~ We paint the shelf. (1)

3. Mom has some grapes. ~~It~~ She puts them in a bowl. (1)

4. My friends come over. ~~We~~ They want to see the shed. (1)

Proofreading Marks	
∧	add
⤷	take out

Words to Know

✏ Circle the word that best completes each sentence.

1. I like (until, (learning)) about animals. (1 point)

2. Our dog Pip is five (follow, (years)) old. (1)

3. Pip has (baby, (eight)) new pups. (1)

4. She will feed her pups ((until,) learning) they are older. (1)

5. A (eight, (young)) kitten came to our home. (1)

6. The new kitten likes to (until, (follow)) Pip. (1)

7. The kitten ((begins,) learning) to think he is Pip's pup! (1)

8. The new kitten is not Pip's (years, (baby)).

Words with *er*, *ir*, *ur*

✏ Read the word. Circle the picture that matches the word.

1. bird (1 point)

2. turn (1)

3. her (1)

4. burn (1)

5. third (1)

6. herd (1)

Words with *er*, *ir*, *ur*

✏ Read the words in the box. Write the word that matches the picture.

clerk	shirt	stir	hurt	curl

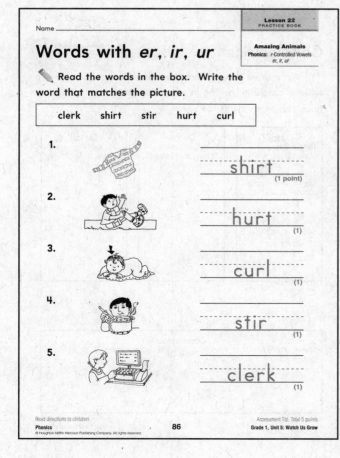

1. shirt (1 point)

2. hurt (1)

3. curl (1)

4. stir (1)

5. clerk (1)

Spelling Words with *r*-Controlled Vowels *er*, *ir*, *ur*

Spelling Words

sir
fern
girl
her
third
hurt
fur
bird
turn
stir

✏ Write the Spelling Words with **er**.

1. her (1 point)   2. fern (1)

✏ Write the Spelling Words with **ir**.

3. girl (1)   4. sir (1)

5. stir (1)   6. bird (1)

7. third (1)

✏ Write the Spelling Words with **ur**.

8. fur (1)   9. hurt (1)

10. turn (1)

Naming Yourself Last

✏️ Circle the correct words to finish each sentence.

1. _____ see the goat.

   Jean and i   (Jean and I) (1 point)

2. _____ pet the sheep.

   I and Steve   (Steve and I) (1)

3. _____ look at the ducks.

   (Rex and I)   i and Rex (1)

✏️ Write the words from the word box to finish the sentence.

Ann	I

4. _____Ann_____ and _____I_____
   hold the baby snakes. (1)

Exact Verbs

✏️ Draw a picture of an animal for a story. Give your animal a name.

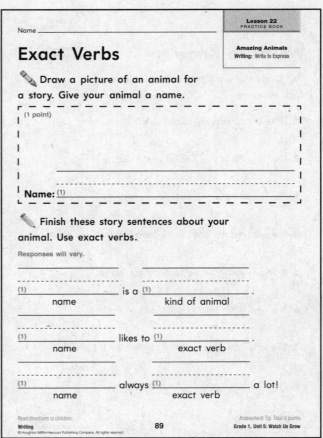

(1 point)

Name: (1) _____

✏️ Finish these story sentences about your animal. Use exact verbs.

Responses will vary.

_____ is a _____ .
(1) name   (1) kind of animal

_____ likes to _____ .
(1) name   (1) exact verb

_____ always _____ a lot!
(1) name   (1) exact verb

Words with er, ir, ur

✏️ Choose a word from the box to name each picture. Write the word.

girl	turn	chirp	third	hers	dirt

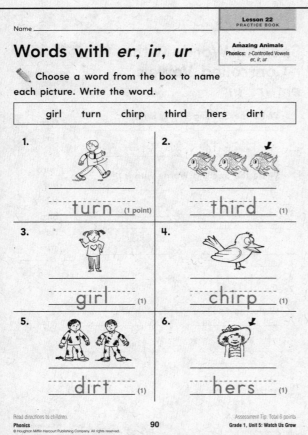

1. turn (1 point)

2. third (1)

3. girl (1)

4. chirp (1)

5. dirt (1)

6. hers (1)

Conclusions

✏️ Write three details from the story. Then write a conclusion telling in what way you think the animals are the same.

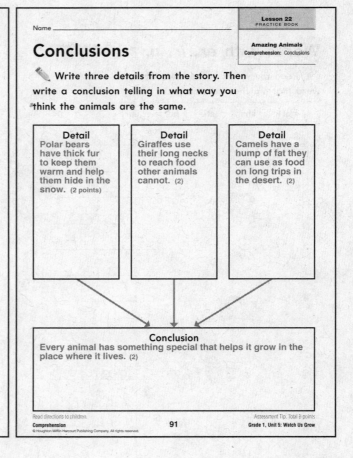

Detail
Polar bears have thick fur to keep them warm and help them hide in the snow. (2 points)

Detail
Giraffes use their long necks to reach food other animals cannot. (2)

Detail
Camels have a hump of fat they can use as food on long trips in the desert. (2)

Conclusion
Every animal has something special that helps it grow in the place where it lives. (2)

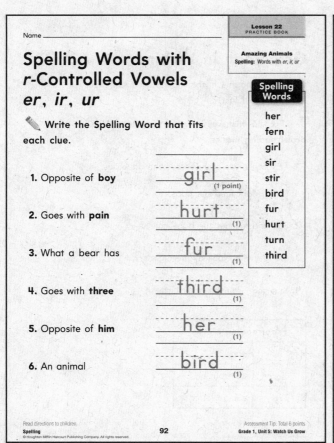

Lesson 22
PRACTICE BOOK

Amazing Animals
Spelling: Words with *er, ir, ur*

Spelling Words with *r*-Controlled Vowels *er*, *ir*, *ur*

Write the Spelling Word that fits each clue.

Spelling Words

her
fern
girl
sir
stir
bird
fur
hurt
turn
third

1. Opposite of **boy** _girl_ (1 point)

2. Goes with **pain** _hurt_ (1)

3. What a bear has _fur_ (1)

4. Goes with **three** _third_ (1)

5. Opposite of **him** _her_ (1)

6. An animal _bird_ (1)

Read directions to children.
Spelling
© Houghton Mifflin Harcourt Publishing Company. All rights reserved.

92

Assessment Tip: Total 6 points
Grade 1, Unit 5: Watch Us Grow

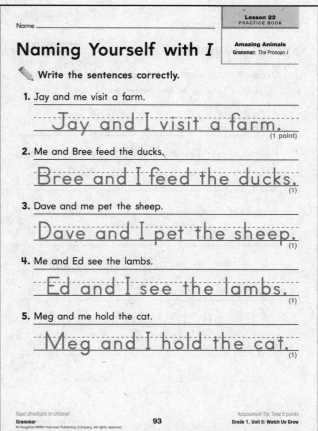

Lesson 22
PRACTICE BOOK

Amazing Animals
Grammar: The Pronoun *I*

Naming Yourself with *I*

Write the sentences correctly.

1. Jay and me visit a farm.
   Jay and I visit a farm. (1 point)

2. Me and Bree feed the ducks.
   Bree and I feed the ducks. (1)

3. Dave and me pet the sheep.
   Dave and I pet the sheep. (1)

4. Me and Ed see the lambs.
   Ed and I see the lambs. (1)

5. Meg and me hold the cat.
   Meg and I hold the cat. (1)

Read directions to children.
Grammar
© Houghton Mifflin Harcourt Publishing Company. All rights reserved.

93

Assessment Tip: Total 5 points
Grade 1, Unit 5: Watch Us Grow

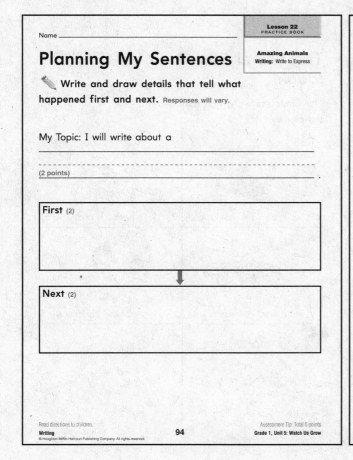

Lesson 22
PRACTICE BOOK

Amazing Animals
Writing: Write to Express

Planning My Sentences

Write and draw details that tell what happened first and next. Responses will vary.

My Topic: I will write about a
_____
- -
(2 points)

First (2)

Next (2)

Read directions to children.
Writing
© Houghton Mifflin Harcourt Publishing Company. All rights reserved.

94

Assessment Tip: Total 6 points
Grade 1, Unit 5: Watch Us Grow

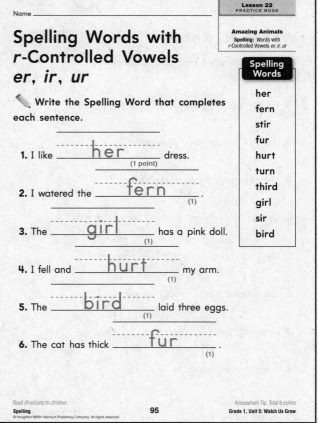

Lesson 22
PRACTICE BOOK

Amazing Animals
Spelling: Words with
r-Controlled Vowels *er, ir, ur*

Spelling Words with *r*-Controlled Vowels *er*, *ir*, *ur*

Write the Spelling Word that completes each sentence.

Spelling Words

her
fern
stir
fur
hurt
turn
third
girl
sir
bird

1. I like _her_ dress. (1 point)

2. I watered the _fern_. (1)

3. The _girl_ has a pink doll. (1)

4. I fell and _hurt_ my arm. (1)

5. The _bird_ laid three eggs. (1)

6. The cat has thick _fur_. (1)

Read directions to children.
Spelling
© Houghton Mifflin Harcourt Publishing Company. All rights reserved.

95

Assessment Tip: Total 6 points
Grade 1, Unit 5: Watch Us Grow

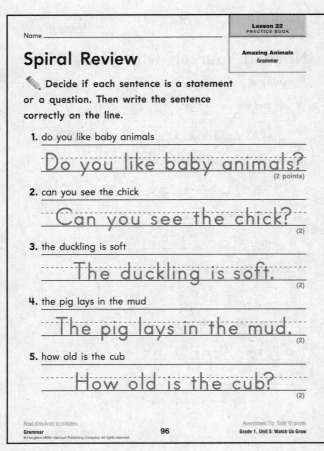

Spiral Review

✏️ Decide if each sentence is a statement or a question. Then write the sentence correctly on the line.

1. do you like baby animals

<u>Do you like baby animals?</u>
(2 points)

2. can you see the chick

<u>Can you see the chick?</u>
(2)

3. the duckling is soft

<u>The duckling is soft.</u>
(2)

4. the pig lays in the mud

<u>The pig lays in the mud.</u>
(2)

5. how old is the cub

<u>How old is the cub?</u>
(2)

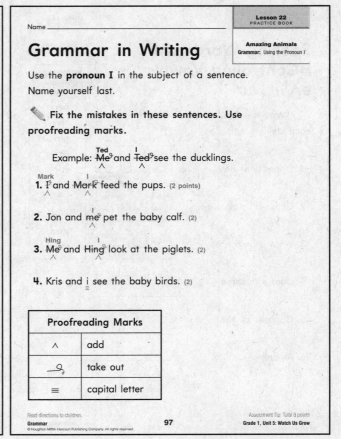

Grammar in Writing

Use the **pronoun I** in the subject of a sentence. Name yourself last.

✏️ Fix the mistakes in these sentences. Use proofreading marks.

Example: ~~Me~~ and ~~Ted~~ see the ducklings.

1. I and Mark feed the pups. (2 points)

2. Jon and me pet the baby calf. (2)

3. Me and Hing look at the piglets. (2)

4. Kris and i see the baby birds. (2)

Proofreading Marks	
∧	add
ℛ	take out
≡	capital letter

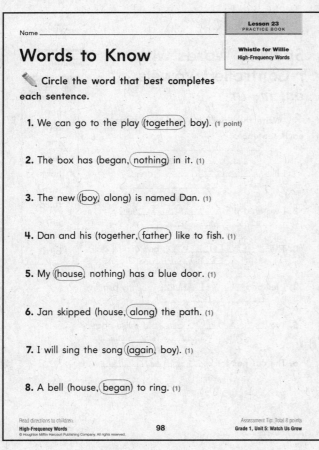

Words to Know

✏️ Circle the word that best completes each sentence.

1. We can go to the play (together, boy). (1 point)

2. The box has (began, nothing) in it. (1)

3. The new (boy, along) is named Dan. (1)

4. Dan and his (together, father) like to fish. (1)

5. My (house, nothing) has a blue door. (1)

6. Jan skipped (house, along) the path. (1)

7. I will sing the song (again, boy). (1)

8. A bell (house, began) to ring. (1)

Name _____

Lesson 23
PRACTICE BOOK

Whistle for Willie
Phonics: Vowel digraph
oo (book)

The Vowel Sound *oo* (book)

✏️ Circle the word that matches the picture.

1. (book) hook (1 point)

2. book (cook) (1)

3. wool (wood) (1)

4. hook (hood) (1)

5. (brook) took (1)

6. soot (foot) (1)

Name _____

Words with *oo* (book)

✎ Circle the sentence that matches the picture.

1. We cook at mealtime.
   (We look at the time.) **(1 point)**

2. (I see a little brook.) **(1)**
   I see a little book.

3. He has a hat made of wool.
   (He has a box made of wood.) **(1)**

4. (Put your coat on a hook.) **(1)**
   Put your coat in a hood.

5. (Wash off that soot.) **(1)**
   Wash off your foot.

© Houghton Mifflin Harcourt Publishing Company. All rights reserved.
Assessment Tip: Total 5 points
Grade 1, Unit 5: Watch Us Grow

Name _____

Spelling Words with Vowel Digraph *oo*

✎ Sort the words. Write the correct Spelling Words in each column.

Spelling Words

look
book
good
hook
brook
took
foot
shook
wood
hood

Words with **ook**	Words with **ood**
look **(1 point)**	good **(1)**
book **(1)**	wood **(1)**
brook **(1)**	hood **(1)**
hook **(1)**	
took **(1)**	
shook **(1)**	

© Houghton Mifflin Harcourt Publishing Company. All rights reserved.
Assessment Tip: Total 9 points
Grade 1, Unit 5: Watch Us Grow

Name _____

Using *my*, *your*, *his*, and *her*

✎ Write the correct pronoun to finish each sentence.

1. I hug ____my____ dog Mags. **(1 point)**

   me   my

2. Mags runs after ____her____ stick. **(1)**

   her   she

3. Rick brings ____his____ dog. **(1)**

   he   his

4. You can bring ____your____ dog, too. **(1)**

   your   you

5. We can play in ____my____ backyard! **(1)**

   they   my

© Houghton Mifflin Harcourt Publishing Company. All rights reserved.
Assessment Tip: Total 5 points
Grade 1, Unit 5: Watch Us Grow

Name _____

Order of Events

✎ Finish the sentences. Give a summary of the first part of **Whistle for Willie**. Responses will vary.

_____

Peter wished **(2 points)** _____

_____

He tried **(2)** _____

When Peter saw Willie, he **(2)** _____

_____

_____

Then, Willie **(2)** _____

_____

© Houghton Mifflin Harcourt Publishing Company. All rights reserved.
Assessment Tip: Total 8 points
Grade 1, Unit 5: Watch Us Grow

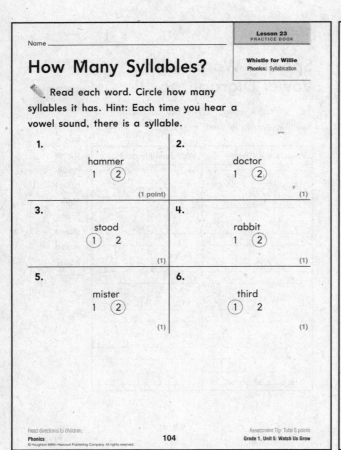

How Many Syllables?

✎ Read each word. Circle how many syllables it has. Hint: Each time you hear a vowel sound, there is a syllable.

1.
hammer
1 ②
(1 point)

2.
doctor
1 ②
(1)

3.
stood
① 2
(1)

4.
rabbit
1 ②
(1)

5.
mister
1 ②
(1)

6.
third
① 2
(1)

Read directions to children.
Phonics
© Houghton Mifflin Harcourt Publishing Company. All rights reserved.
104
Assessment Tip: Total 6 points
Grade 1, Unit 5: Watch Us Grow

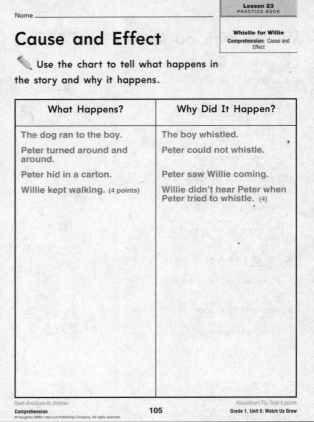

Cause and Effect

✎ Use the chart to tell what happens in the story and why it happens.

What Happens?	Why Did It Happen?
The dog ran to the boy.	The boy whistled.
Peter turned around and around.	Peter could not whistle.
Peter hid in a carton.	Peter saw Willie coming.
Willie kept walking. (4 points)	Willie didn't hear Peter when Peter tried to whistle. (4)

Read directions to children.
Comprehension
© Houghton Mifflin Harcourt Publishing Company. All rights reserved.
105
Assessment Tip: Total 8 points
Grade 1, Unit 5: Watch Us Grow

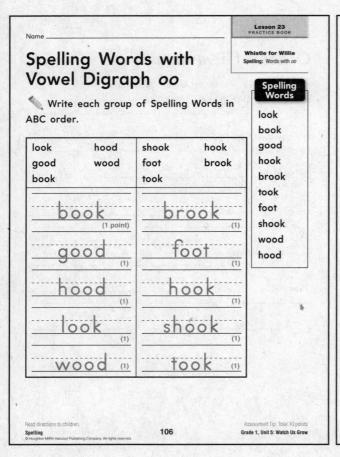

Spelling Words with Vowel Digraph *oo*

✎ Write each group of Spelling Words in ABC order.

Spelling Words
look
book
good
hook
brook
took
foot
shook
wood
hood

look	hood	shook	hook
good	wood	foot	brook
book		took	

book (1 point)

brook (1)

good (1)

foot (1)

hood (1)

hook (1)

look (1)

shook (1)

wood (1)

took (1)

Read directions to children.
Spelling
© Houghton Mifflin Harcourt Publishing Company. All rights reserved.
106
Assessment Tip: Total 10 points
Grade 1, Unit 5: Watch Us Grow

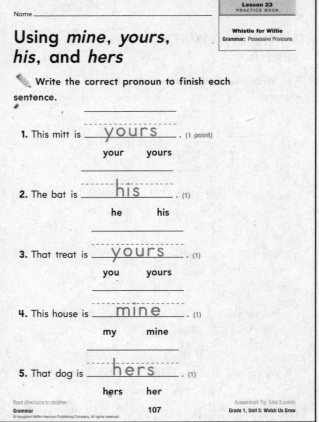

Using *mine*, *yours*, *his*, and *hers*

✎ Write the correct pronoun to finish each sentence.

1. This mitt is _yours_ . (1 point)
your   yours

2. The bat is _his_ . (1)
he   his

3. That treat is _yours_ . (1)
you   yours

4. This house is _mine_ . (1)
my   mine

5. That dog is _hers_ . (1)
hers   her

Read directions to children.
Grammar
© Houghton Mifflin Harcourt Publishing Company. All rights reserved.
107
Assessment Tip: Total 5 points
Grade 1, Unit 5: Watch Us Grow

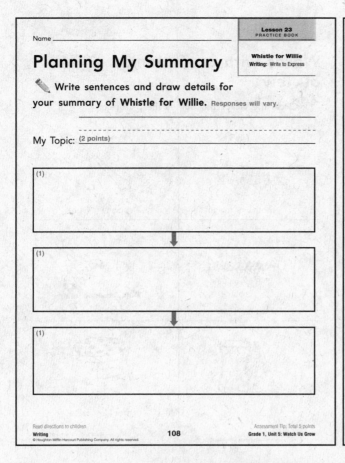

Planning My Summary

✏️ Write sentences and draw details for your summary of **Whistle for Willie.** Responses will vary.

_____

My Topic: (2 points) _____

(1)

(1)

(1)

Read directions to children.
Writing
© Houghton Mifflin Harcourt Publishing Company. All rights reserved.
108
Assessment Tip: Total 5 points
Grade 1, Unit 5: Watch Us Grow

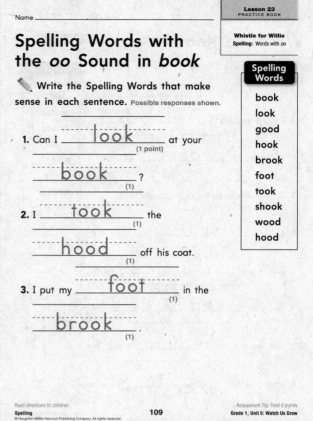

Spelling Words with the *oo* Sound in *book*

✏️ Write the Spelling Words that make sense in each sentence. Possible responses shown.

Spelling Words
book
look
good
hook
brook
foot
took
shook
wood
hood

1. Can I _____ look _____ at your (1 point)

_____ book _____ ?
(1)

2. I _____ took _____ the
(1)

_____ hood _____ off his coat.
(1)

3. I put my _____ foot _____ in the
(1)

_____ brook _____ .
(1)

Read directions to children.
Spelling
© Houghton Mifflin Harcourt Publishing Company. All rights reserved.
109
Assessment Tip: Total 6 points
Grade 1, Unit 5: Watch Us Grow

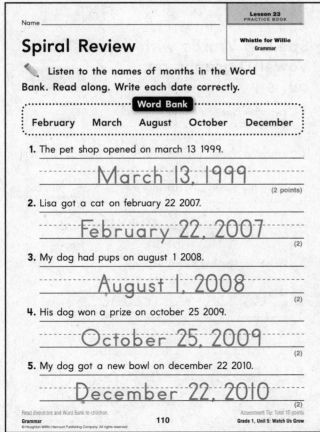

Spiral Review

✏️ Listen to the names of months in the Word Bank. Read along. Write each date correctly.

Word Bank
February   March   August   October   December

1. The pet shop opened on march 13 1999.

March 13, 1999
(2 points)

2. Lisa got a cat on february 22 2007.

February 22, 2007
(2)

3. My dog had pups on august 1 2008.

August 1, 2008
(2)

4. His dog won a prize on october 25 2009.

October 25, 2009
(2)

5. My dog got a new bowl on december 22 2010.

December 22, 2010
(2)

Read directions and Word Bank to children.
Grammar
© Houghton Mifflin Harcourt Publishing Company. All rights reserved.
110
Assessment Tip: Total 10 points
Grade 1, Unit 5: Watch Us Grow

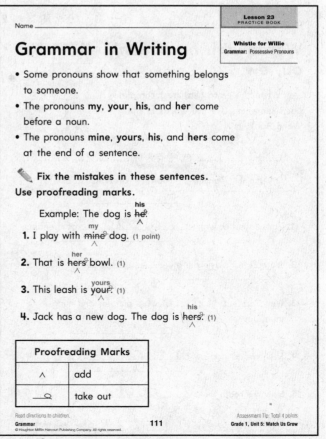

Grammar in Writing

- Some pronouns show that something belongs to someone.
- The pronouns **my, your, his,** and **her** come before a noun.
- The pronouns **mine, yours, his,** and **hers** come at the end of a sentence.

✏️ Fix the mistakes in these sentences. Use proofreading marks.

Example: The dog is ~~her~~ his.

1. I play with ~~mine~~ my dog. (1 point)

2. That is ~~hers~~ her bowl. (1)

3. This leash is ~~your~~ yours. (1)

4. Jack has a new dog. The dog is ~~hers~~ his. (1)

Proofreading Marks	
∧	add
◯	take out

Read directions to children.
Grammar
© Houghton Mifflin Harcourt Publishing Company. All rights reserved.
111
Assessment Tip: Total 4 points
Grade 1, Unit 5: Watch Us Grow

Words to Know

✏️ Write a word from the box to complete each sentence.

Words to Know

also
anything
flower
kind
places
ready
upon
warm

1. I want to pick the __flower__ (1 point)

2. It is very __warm__ outside. (1)

3. Cats sleep in soft __places__ . (1)

4. Nate __also__ likes ice cream. (1)

5. Tag is one __kind__ of game. (1)

6. Are you __ready__ to go? (1)

7. Lee reads __anything__ about bugs. (1)

8. I put the hat __upon__ my head. (1)

Read directions to children.
High-Frequency Words
© Houghton Mifflin Harcourt Publishing Company. All rights reserved.
112
Assessment Tip: Total 8 points
Grade 1, Unit 5: Watch Us Grow

Words with *oo* (moon), *ou*, *ew*

✏️ Circle the word that names the picture.

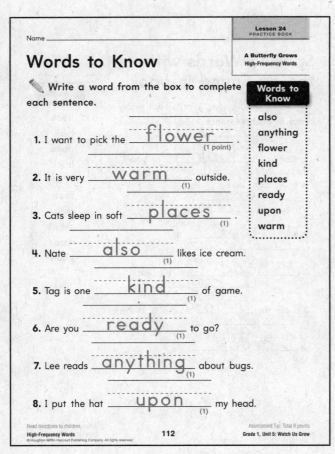

1. moth (moon) (1 point)

2. (spoon) spot (1)

3. scream (screw) (1)

4. soap (soup) (1)

5. boat (boot) (1)

6. (stool) stole (1)

Read directions to children.
Phonics
© Houghton Mifflin Harcourt Publishing Company. All rights reserved.
113
Assessment Tip: Total 6 points
Grade 1, Unit 5: Watch Us Grow

Words with *oo* (moon), *ou*, *ew*

✏️ Write the word that best completes each sentence. Use the words in the Word Bank.

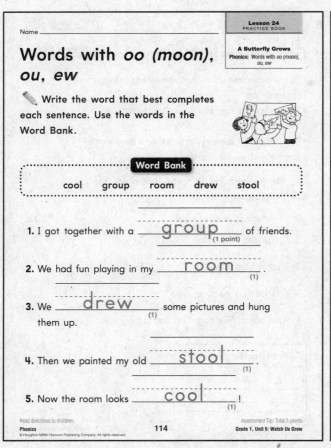

Word Bank

cool   group   room   drew   stool

1. I got together with a __group__ of friends. (1 point)

2. We had fun playing in my __room__ . (1)

3. We __drew__ some pictures and hung them up. (1)

4. Then we painted my old __stool__ . (1)

5. Now the room looks __cool__ ! (1)

Read directions to children.
Phonics
© Houghton Mifflin Harcourt Publishing Company. All rights reserved.
114
Assessment Tip: Total 5 points
Grade 1, Unit 5: Watch Us Grow

Spelling Words with Vowel Digraphs *oo*, *ou*, *ew*

✏️ Write the Spelling Words with **ou**.

Spelling Words

soon
new
noon
zoo
boot
too
moon
blew
soup
you

1. __soup__ (1 point)   2. __you__ (1)

✏️ Write the Spelling Words with **ew**.

3. __new__ (1)   4. __blew__ (1)

✏️ Write the Spelling Words with **oo**.

5. __soon__ (1)   6. __noon__ (1)

7. __zoo__ (1)   8. __boot__ (1)

9. __too__ (1)   10. __moon__ (1)

Read directions to children.
Spelling
© Houghton Mifflin Harcourt Publishing Company. All rights reserved.
115
Assessment Tip: Total 10 points
Grade 1, Unit 5: Watch Us Grow

Lesson 24
PRACTICE BOOK

Pronouns and Action Verbs

A Butterfly Grows
Grammar: Pronouns and Verbs

✏️ Write the correct verb to finish each sentence about a **caterpillar** and a **butterfly**.

1. Jill _____looks_____ at the leaf. (1 point)

   look   looks

2. She _____sees_____ a **caterpillar**. (1)

   sees   see

3. It _____gets_____ bigger and bigger. (1)

   get   gets

4. It _____turns_____ into a **butterfly!** (1)

   turns   turn

5. She _____claps_____ her hands. (1)

   clap   claps

116   Assessment Tip: Total 5 points

Grade 1, Unit 5: Watch Us Grow

Lesson 24
PRACTICE BOOK

Describing Characters

A Butterfly Grows
Writing: Write to Express

✏️ Write clear details to finish the story.
Some details should describe Rex and Grace.
Sentences will vary.

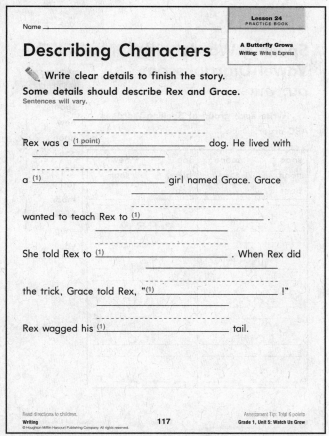

Rex was a (1 point) _____ dog. He lived with

a (1) _____ girl named Grace. Grace

wanted to teach Rex to (1) _____ .

She told Rex to (1) _____ . When Rex did

the trick, Grace told Rex, "(1)_____ !"

Rex wagged his (1) _____ tail.

117   Assessment Tip: Total 6 points

Grade 1, Unit 5: Watch Us Grow

Lesson 24
PRACTICE BOOK

Words with *ue, u, u_e*

A Butterfly Grows
Phonics: Words with *ue, u, u_e*

✏️ Circle the two words in each row that have the same vowel sound.
Write the letters that spell the sound.

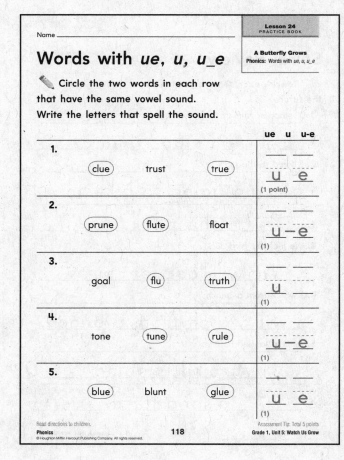

				ue	u	u-e
1.	(clue)	trust	(true)		u_e	(1 point)
2.	(prune)	(flute)	float		u-e	(1)
3.	goal	(flu)	(truth)	u		(1)
4.	tone	(tune)	(rule)		u-e	(1)
5.	(blue)	blunt	(glue)	u e		(1)

118   Assessment Tip: Total 5 points

Grade 1, Unit 5: Watch Us Grow

Lesson 24
PRACTICE BOOK

Sequence of Events

A Butterfly Grows
Comprehension: Sequence of Events

✏️ Write about things that happen in **A Butterfly Grows**. Put the events in order.

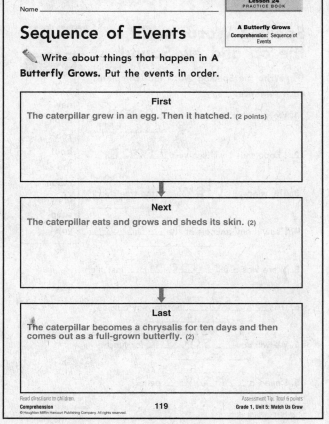

First
The caterpillar grew in an egg. Then it hatched. (2 points)

Next
The caterpillar eats and grows and sheds its skin. (2)

Last
The caterpillar becomes a chrysalis for ten days and then comes out as a full-grown butterfly. (2)

119   Assessment Tip: Total 6 points

Grade 1, Unit 5: Watch Us Grow

A Butterfly Grows
Spelling: Words with oo, ou, ew

Spelling Words with Vowel Digraphs *oo*, *ou*, *ew*

✏️ Write each group of Spelling Words in ABC order.

Spelling Words

soon
new
noon
zoo
boot
too
moon
blew
soup
you

soon	moon	too	new
noon	zoo	blew	soup
boot		you	

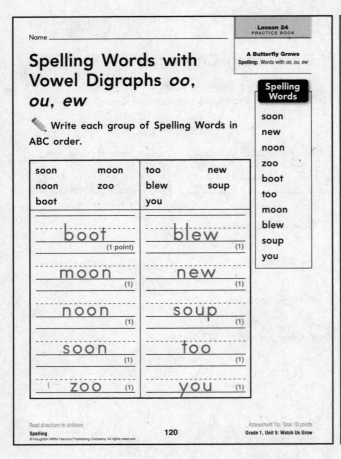

boot (1 point)   blew (1)

moon (1)   new (1)

noon (1)   soup (1)

soon (1)   too (1)

zoo (1)   you (1)

Read directions to children.
Spelling
© Houghton Mifflin Harcourt Publishing Company. All rights reserved.
120
Assessment Tip: Total 10 points
Grade 1, Unit 5: Watch Us Grow

A Butterfly Grows
Grammar: Pronouns and Verbs

Pronouns and *be*

✏️ Write the correct verb to finish each sentence.

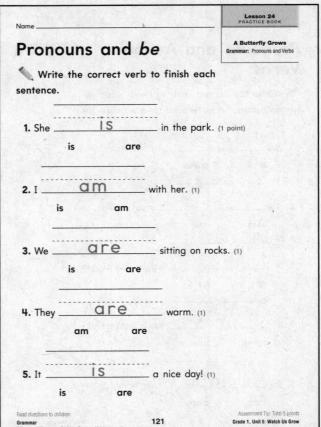

1. She _____ is _____ in the park. (1 point)

    is   are

2. I _____ am _____ with her. (1)

    is   am

3. We _____ are _____ sitting on rocks. (1)

    is   are

4. They _____ are _____ warm. (1)

    am   are

5. It _____ is _____ a nice day! (1)

    is   are

Read directions to children.
Grammar
© Houghton Mifflin Harcourt Publishing Company. All rights reserved.
121
Assessment Tip: Total 5 points
Grade 1, Unit 5: Watch Us Grow

A Butterfly Grows
Spelling: Words with oo and ew

Spelling Words with the *oo* and *ew* Sound

✏️ Write the Spelling Word that completes each sentence.

Spelling Words

soon
new
noon
zoo
boot
too
moon
blew
soup
you

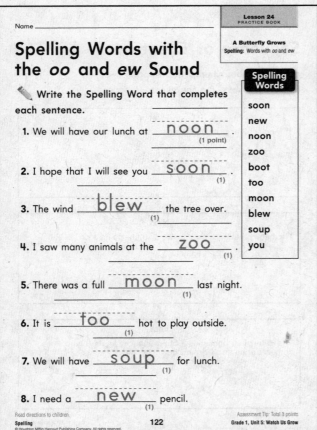

1. We will have our lunch at ___ noon ___ (1 point)

2. I hope that I will see you ___ soon ___ (1)

3. The wind ___ blew ___ the tree over. (1)

4. I saw many animals at the ___ zoo ___ . (1)

5. There was a full ___ moon ___ last night. (1)

6. It is ___ too ___ hot to play outside. (1)

7. We will have ___ soup ___ for lunch. (1)

8. I need a ___ new ___ pencil. (1)

Read directions to children.
Spelling
© Houghton Mifflin Harcourt Publishing Company. All rights reserved.
122
Assessment Tip: Total 8 points
Grade 1, Unit 5: Watch Us Grow

A Butterfly Grows
Grammar

Spiral Review

✏️ Rewrite each sentence to tell about the future.

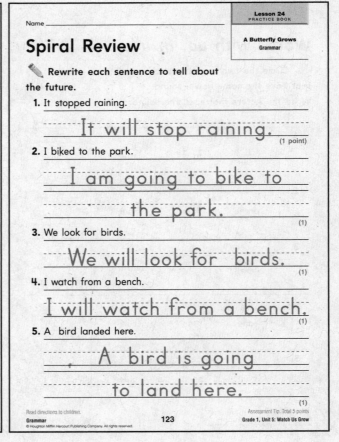

1. It stopped raining.

It will stop raining. (1 point)

2. I biked to the park.

I am going to bike to the park. (1)

3. We look for birds.

We will look for birds. (1)

4. I watch from a bench.

I will watch from a bench. (1)

5. A bird landed here.

A bird is going to land here. (1)

Read directions to children.
Grammar
© Houghton Mifflin Harcourt Publishing Company. All rights reserved.
123
Assessment Tip: Total 5 points
Grade 1, Unit 5: Watch Us Grow

Lesson 24
PRACTICE BOOK

A Butterfly Grows
Writing: Write to Express

Planning My Story

✎ Write and draw details for your story.

Responses will vary.

Characters (1 point)	Setting (1)

Plot
Beginning (1)
Middle (1)
End (1)

Read directions to children.
Writing
© Houghton Mifflin Harcourt Publishing Company. All rights reserved.
124
Assessment Tip: Total 5 points
Grade 1, Unit 5: Watch Us Grow

Lesson 24
PRACTICE BOOK

A Butterfly Grows
Grammar: Pronouns and Verbs

Grammar in Writing

- Add **s** to most **verbs** when they tell about a pronoun that names one.
- Use **am** with the pronoun **I**. Use **is** with pronouns that name one. Use **are** with pronouns that name more than one.

✎ Fix the mistakes in these sentences.
Use proofreading marks.

Example: We ~~is~~ in the park. ^are^

1. We sees^see^ many flowers. (2 points)

2. They am^are^ pretty. (2)

3. I calls^call^ my friend. (2)

4. She give^gives^ me a big smile. (2)

Proofreading Marks	
∧	add
⌐	take out

Read directions to children.
Grammar
© Houghton Mifflin Harcourt Publishing Company. All rights reserved.
125
Assessment Tip: Total 8 points
Grade 1, Unit 5: Watch Us Grow

Lesson 25
PRACTICE BOOK

The New Friend
High-Frequency Words

Words to Know

✎ Draw a line to match each picture to the word that goes with it.

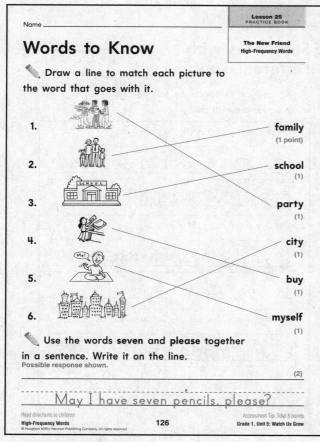

1. family (1 point)
2. school (1)
3. party (1)
4. city (1)
5. buy (1)
6. myself (1)

✎ Use the words **seven** and **please** together in a sentence. Write it on the line.
Possible response shown. (2)

May I have seven pencils, please?

Read directions to children
High-Frequency Words
© Houghton Mifflin Harcourt Publishing Company. All rights reserved.
126
Assessment Tip: Total 8 points
Grade 1, Unit 5: Watch Us Grow

Lesson 25
PRACTICE BOOK

The New Friend
Phonics: Words with ou, ow

Words with *ou, ow*

✎ Circle the word that names the picture.

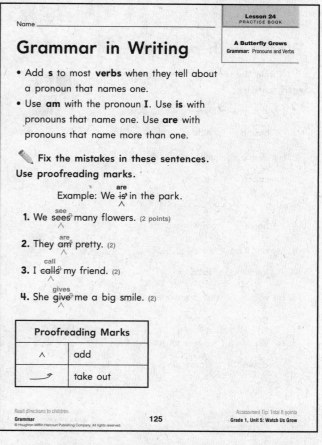

1. cot (cow) (1 point)
2. (couch) coach (1)
3. moose (mouse) (1)
4. crow (crown) (1)
5. plate (plow) (1)
6. (cloud) closed (1)

Read directions to children.
Phonics
© Houghton Mifflin Harcourt Publishing Company. All rights reserved.
127
Assessment Tip: Total 6 points
Grade 1, Unit 5: Watch Us Grow

Words with *ou, ow*

✏️ Circle the word that best completes each sentence.

1. I got a new pet. He's a _____ dog.
   (**hound**)   **hold** (1 point)

2. He should not jump up on the _____.
   coach   (**couch**) (1)

3. At night, my dog _____ at the moon.
   holes   (**howls**) (1)

4. My dog's bark is very _____.
   (**loud**)   **load** (1)

5. He will _____ when someone comes to the house!
   grow   (**growl**) (1)

6. He sits when I tell him to get _____.
   (**down**)   **dome** (1)

Read directions to children.
Phonics
© Houghton Mifflin Harcourt Publishing Company. All rights reserved.
128
Assessment Tip: Total 6 points
Grade 1, Unit 5: Watch Us Grow

Spelling Words with Vowel Diphthongs *ow, ou*

✏️ Sort the words. Write the correct Spelling Words in each column.

Spelling Words

how
now
cow
owl
ouch
house
found
out
gown
town

Words with **ou**	Words with **ow**
ouch (1 point)	how (1)
house (1)	now (1)
found (1)	cow (1)
out (1)	owl
	gown (1)
	town (1)

Read directions to children.
Spelling
© Houghton Mifflin Harcourt Publishing Company. All rights reserved.
129
Assessment Tip: Total 10 points
Grade 1, Unit 5: Watch Us Grow

Contractions with *not*

✏️ Write a contraction from the box for the underlined word or words.

Word Bank

isn't
aren't
can't
don't

1. This house <u>is not</u> empty now.

   _____ isn't _____ (1 point)

2. I <u>do not</u> know where my books are.

   _____ don't _____ (1)

3. They <u>are not</u> in this big box.

   _____ aren't _____ (1)

4. I <u>cannot</u> find my jump rope.

   _____ can't _____ (1)

5. I <u>do not</u> have a new friend yet.

   _____ don't _____ (1)

Read directions to children.
Grammar
© Houghton Mifflin Harcourt Publishing Company. All rights reserved.
130
Assessment Tip: Total 5 points
Grade 1, Unit 5: Watch Us Grow

Sentences with Different Lengths

✏️ Make long sentences by joining two short sentences with **and**.

1. Kirk moved to a new city. He was happy.

   Kirk moved to a new city , (1)
   and he was happy (1)

2. The city is far away. It is very big.

   The city is far away , (1)
   and it is very big (1)

3. Kirk made new friends. He saw new places.

   Kirk made new friends , (1)
   and he saw new places (1)

Read directions to children.
Writing
© Houghton Mifflin Harcourt Publishing Company. All rights reserved.
131
Assessment Tip: Total 6 points
Grade 1, Unit 5: Watch Us Grow

Words with *oi*, *oy*, *au*, *aw*

✏️ Circle the two words in each row that have the same vowel sound. Write the letters that spell the sound.

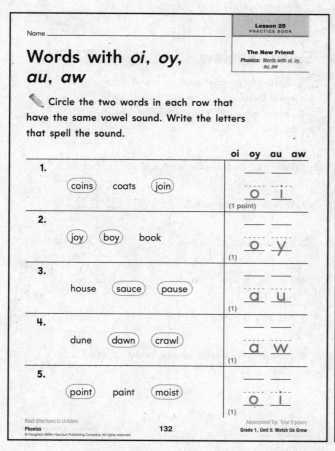

		oi oy au aw
1.	(coins) coats (join)	o i (1 point)
2.	(joy) (boy) book	o y (1)
3.	house (sauce) (pause)	a u (1)
4.	dune (dawn) (crawl)	a w (1)
5.	(point) paint (moist)	o i (1)

Read directions to children.
Phonics
© Houghton Mifflin Harcourt Publishing Company. All rights reserved.
132
Assessment Tip: Total 5 points
Grade 1, Unit 5: Watch Us Grow

Understanding Characters

✏️ Write or draw things the boys said in the story in the **Speaking** box. Write or draw things the boys did in the **Acting** box. Write or draw about the feelings of the boys in the **Feeling** box.

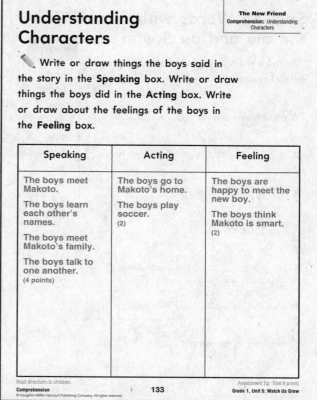

Speaking	Acting	Feeling
The boys meet Makoto. The boys learn each other's names. The boys meet Makoto's family. The boys talk to one another. (4 points)	The boys go to Makoto's home. The boys play soccer. (2)	The boys are happy to meet the new boy. The boys think Makoto is smart. (2)

Read directions to children.
Comprehension
© Houghton Mifflin Harcourt Publishing Company. All rights reserved.
133
Assessment Tip: Total 8 points
Grade 1, Unit 5: Watch Us Grow

Spelling Words with Vowel Diphthongs *ou*, *ow*

✏️ Write the Spelling Word that fits each clue.

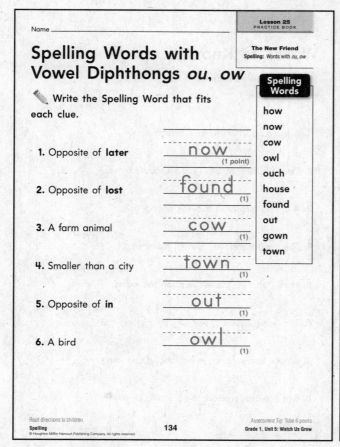

Spelling Words

how
now
cow
owl
ouch
house
found
out
gown
town

1. Opposite of **later**   now (1 point)

2. Opposite of **lost**   found (1)

3. A farm animal   cow (1)

4. Smaller than a city   town (1)

5. Opposite of **in**   out (1)

6. A bird   owl (1)

Read directions to children.
Spelling
© Houghton Mifflin Harcourt Publishing Company. All rights reserved.
134
Assessment Tip: Total 6 points
Grade 1, Unit 5: Watch Us Grow

Contractions with Pronouns

✏️ Write a contraction from the box for the underlined words.

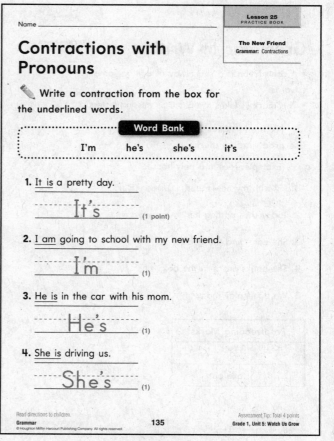

Word Bank

I'm   he's   she's   it's

1. <u>It is</u> a pretty day.

It's (1 point)

2. <u>I am</u> going to school with my new friend.

I'm (1)

3. <u>He is</u> in the car with his mom.

He's (1)

4. <u>She is</u> driving us.

She's (1)

Read directions to children.
Grammar
© Houghton Mifflin Harcourt Publishing Company. All rights reserved.
135
Assessment Tip: Total 4 points
Grade 1, Unit 5: Watch Us Grow

Lesson 25
PRACTICE BOOK

The New Friend
Spelling: Words with *ow* and *ou*

Spelling Words with the *ow* and *ou* Sound

✏️ Write the Spelling Word that completes each sentence.

Spelling Words

how
house
now
owl
cow
found
town
ouch
out
gown

1. We're walking to my ___house___ . (1 point)

2. ___How___ will you get home? (1)

3. Do you live far from ___town___ ? (1)

4. I'm going ___out___ to play. (1)

5. ___Ouch___ ! That hurt! (1)

6. He's coming home right ___now___ . (1)

Read directions to children.
Spelling
© Houghton Mifflin Harcourt Publishing Company. All rights reserved.
136
Assessment Tip: Total 6 points
Grade 1, Unit 5: Watch Us Grow

Lesson 25
PRACTICE BOOK

The New Friend
Grammar

Spiral Review

✏️ Circle the prepositional phrase in each sentence. Decide if the prepositional phrase tells where or when. Write **where** or **when** on the line.

1. Max and Viv play (after school.) ___when___ (1 point)

2. They meet (in the park.) ___where___ (1)

3. Viv's kite is stuck (in a tree.) ___where___ (1)

4. They race (on the grass.) ___where___ (1)

5. The park closes (at five o'clock.) ___when___ (1)

6. The friends will meet again (next week.) ___when___ (1)

Read directions to children.
Grammar
© Houghton Mifflin Harcourt Publishing Company. All rights reserved.
137
Assessment Tip: Total 6 points
Grade 1, Unit 5: Watch Us Grow

Lesson 25
PRACTICE BOOK

The New Friend
Grammar: Contractions

Grammar in Writing

- A contraction is a short way of writing some words.
- This mark (') takes the place of missing letters.

✏️ Fix the mistakes in these sentences.
Use proofreading marks.

Example: He's
Hes in a new house.
       ∧

1. I'm with my new friend. (2 points)

2. Today she's putting her toys away. (2)

3. She can't find the games. (2)

4. The books aren't in the box. (2)

5. We don't play today. (2)

Proofreading Marks	
∧	add
⤸	take out

Read directions to children.
Grammar
© Houghton Mifflin Harcourt Publishing Company. All rights reserved.
138
Assessment Tip: Total 10 points
Grade 1, Unit 5: Watch Us Grow

Lesson 26
PRACTICE BOOK

The Dot
High-Frequency Words

Words to Know

✏️ Circle the correct word to complete each sentence.

1. A (even, (teacher)) helps you learn. (1 point)

2. Please push that box ((toward,) pushed) me. (1)

3. A ((bear,) surprised) is a big animal. (1)

4. The lamp is ((above,) pushed) the shelf. (1)

5. Mom (teacher, (pushed)) Kim on the swing. (1)

6. Jim was ((surprised,) even) by his birthday gift. (1)

7. All the family came, ((even,) above) Grandma. (1)

8. Ben (toward, (studied)) the painting closely. (1)

Read directions to children
High-Frequency Words
© Houghton Mifflin Harcourt Publishing Company. All rights reserved.
139
Assessment Tip: Total 8 points
Grade 1, Unit 6: Three Cheers for Us!

Adding -ed, -ing

✏️ Look at the picture. Read the word. Circle the **-ed** or **-ing** word that is spelled correctly.

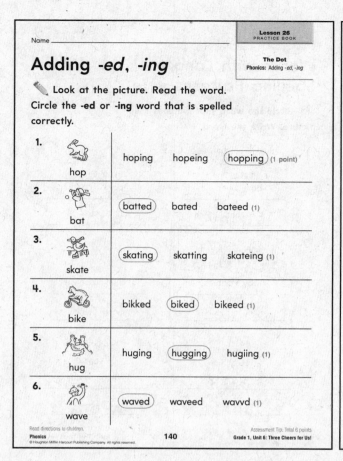

1. hop — hoping · hopeing · (hopping) (1 point)
2. bat — (batted) · bated · bateed (1)
3. skate — (skating) · skatting · skateing (1)
4. bike — bikked · (biked) · bikeed (1)
5. hug — huging · (hugging) · hugiing (1)
6. wave — (waved) · waveed · wavvd (1)

Read directions to children.
Phonics
© Houghton Mifflin Harcourt Publishing Company. All rights reserved.

140

Assessment Tip: Total 6 points
Grade 1, Unit 6: Three Cheers for Us!

Adding -ed, -ing

✏️ Circle the word that fits in the sentence.

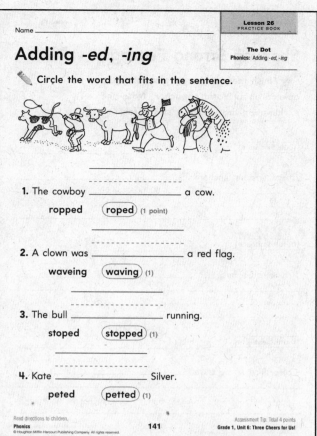

1. The cowboy _____ a cow.
   ropped · (roped) (1 point)

2. A clown was _____ a red flag.
   waveing · (waving) (1)

3. The bull _____ running.
   stoped · (stopped) (1)

4. Kate _____ Silver.
   peted · (petted) (1)

Read directions to children.
Phonics
© Houghton Mifflin Harcourt Publishing Company. All rights reserved.

141

Assessment Tip: Total 4 points
Grade 1, Unit 6: Three Cheers for Us!

Spelling Words Ending in -ed, -ing

✏️ Write the Spelling Words that end in **-ing**.

Spelling Words
mix
mixed
hop
hopped
hope
hoping
run
running
use
used

1. hoping (1 point)   2. running (1)

✏️ Write the Spelling Words that end in **-ed**.

3. mixed (1)   4. hopped (1)

5. used (1)

✏️ Write the Spelling Words that are base words.

6. mix (1)   7. hop (1)

8. hope (1)   9. run (1)

10. use (1)

Read directions to children.
Spelling
© Houghton Mifflin Harcourt Publishing Company. All rights reserved.

142

Assessment Tip: Total 10 points
Grade 1, Unit 6: Three Cheers for Us!

What Is an Exclamation?

✏️ Draw a line under each exclamation.

1. The art show was great! (1 point)
   I saw many paintings.

2. Did you see the painting of the dog?
   I liked that one the most! (1)

3. Dee and Jan put the show together.
   They did a good job! (1)

4. I hope our class can see that show! (1)
   Don't you think so, too?

5. Kay saw the show yesterday.
   She wants to see it again! (1)

Read directions to children.
Grammar
© Houghton Mifflin Harcourt Publishing Company. All rights reserved.

143

Assessment Tip: Total 5 points
Grade 1, Unit 6: Three Cheers for Us!

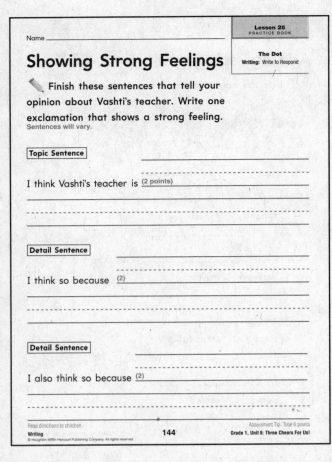

Name _____

Showing Strong Feelings

✏️ Finish these sentences that tell your opinion about Vashti's teacher. Write one exclamation that shows a strong feeling.
Sentences will vary.

Lesson 26
PRACTICE BOOK

The Dot
Writing: Write to Respond

| Topic Sentence | _____ |

I think Vashti's teacher is (2 points)
_____
- -

| Detail Sentence | _____ |

I think so because (2)
_____
- -

| Detail Sentence | _____ |

I also think so because (2)
_____
- -

144

Name _____

Words with Long *e* Spelling Patterns *y, ie*

Lesson 26
PRACTICE BOOK

The Dot
Phonics: Long *e* Spelling Patterns *y, ie*

✏️ Circle the word that matches the picture. Write the word.

1. bus (bunny)
   bunny (1 point)

2. park (party)
   party (1)

3. baby (babies)
   babies (1)

4. (chief) cheese
   chief (1)

5. (sunny) seed
   sunny (1)

6. when (windy)
   windy (1)

145

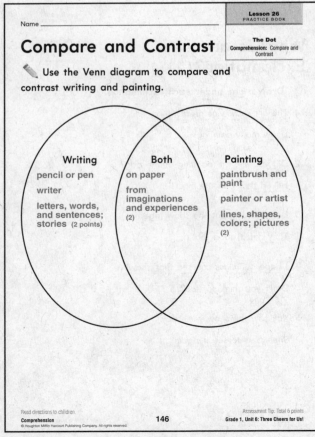

Name _____

Compare and Contrast

Lesson 26
PRACTICE BOOK

The Dot
Comprehension: Compare and Contrast

✏️ Use the Venn diagram to compare and contrast writing and painting.

Writing
pencil or pen
writer
letters, words, and sentences; stories (2 points)

Both
on paper
from imaginations and experiences (2)

Painting
paintbrush and paint
painter or artist
lines, shapes, colors; pictures (2)

146

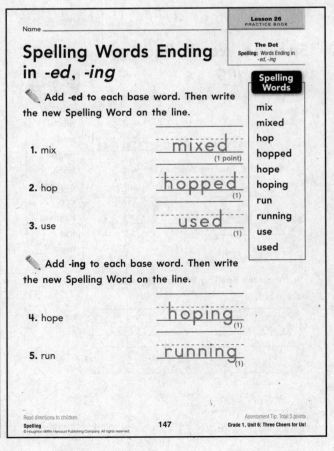

Name _____

Spelling Words Ending in *-ed*, *-ing*

Lesson 26
PRACTICE BOOK

The Dot
Spelling: Words Ending in *-ed, -ing*

✏️ Add **-ed** to each base word. Then write the new Spelling Word on the line.

1. mix   **mixed** (1 point)

2. hop   **hopped** (1)

3. use   **used** (1)

✏️ Add **-ing** to each base word. Then write the new Spelling Word on the line.

4. hope   **hoping** (1)

5. run   **running** (1)

Spelling Words

mix
mixed
hop
hopped
hope
hoping
run
running
use
used

147

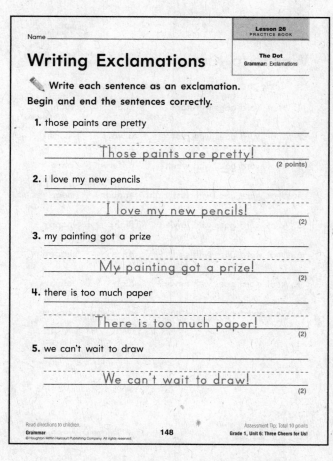

Writing Exclamations

The Dot
Grammar: Exclamations

Write each sentence as an exclamation.
Begin and end the sentences correctly.

1. those paints are pretty

<u>Those paints are pretty!</u>

(2 points)

2. i love my new pencils

<u>I love my new pencils!</u>

(2)

3. my painting got a prize

<u>My painting got a prize!</u>

(2)

4. there is too much paper

<u>There is too much paper!</u>

(2)

5. we can't wait to draw

<u>We can't wait to draw!</u>

(2)

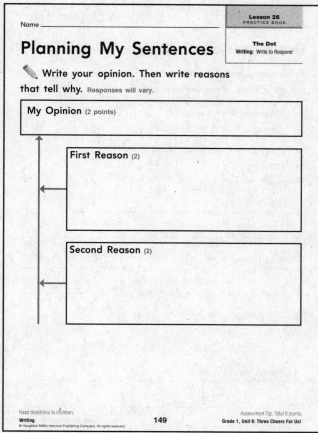

Planning My Sentences

The Dot
Writing: Write to Respond

Write your opinion. Then write reasons
that tell why. Responses will vary.

My Opinion (2 points)

First Reason (2)

Second Reason (2)

Words with Endings -ed and -ing

The Dot
Spelling: Words with -ed and -ing

Write the Spelling Word to complete
each sentence.

1. The bunny <u>hopped</u> away.
(1 point)
(hop, hopped)

2. I <u>hope</u> I will win the race.
(1)
(hope, hoping)

3. He is <u>running</u> very fast.
(1)
(run, running)

4. Kim <u>used</u> all the glue in her art project.
(1)
(use, used)

5. I <u>mixed</u> the eggs and the butter.
(1)
(mix, mixed)

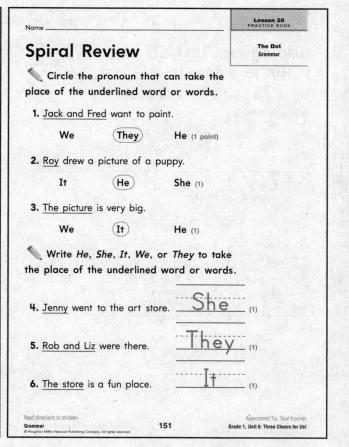

Spiral Review

The Dot
Grammar

Circle the pronoun that can take the
place of the underlined word or words.

1. <u>Jack and Fred</u> want to paint.

We   (They)   He (1 point)

2. <u>Roy</u> drew a picture of a puppy.

It   (He)   She (1)

3. <u>The picture</u> is very big.

We   (It)   He (1)

Write He, She, It, We, or They to take
the place of the underlined word or words.

4. <u>Jenny</u> went to the art store.   <u>She</u> (1)

5. <u>Rob and Liz</u> were there.   <u>They</u> (1)

6. <u>The store</u> is a fun place.   <u>It</u> (1)

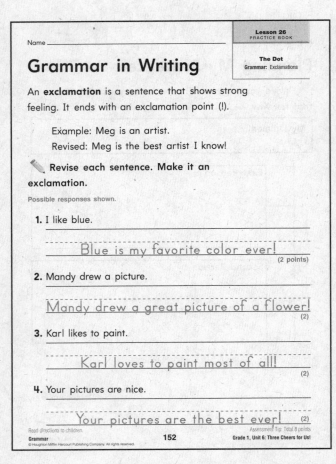

Grammar in Writing

An **exclamation** is a sentence that shows strong feeling. It ends with an exclamation point (!).

Example: Meg is an artist.
Revised: Meg is the best artist I know!

Revise each sentence. Make it an exclamation.

Possible responses shown.

1. I like blue.

   Blue is my favorite color ever!
   (2 points)

2. Mandy drew a picture.

   Mandy drew a great picture of a flower!
   (2)

3. Karl likes to paint.

   Karl loves to paint most of all!
   (2)

4. Your pictures are nice.

   Your pictures are the best ever! (2)

Read directions to children.
Grammar
152

Assessment Tip: Total 8 points
Grade 1, Unit 6: Three Cheers for Us!

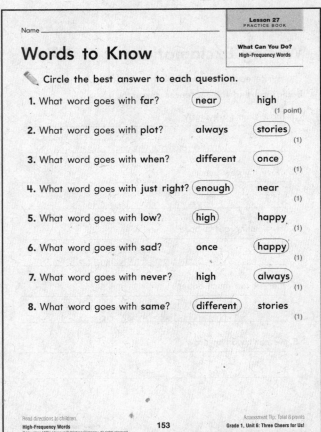

Words to Know

Circle the best answer to each question.

1. What word goes with **far**? (near) high
   (1 point)

2. What word goes with **plot**? always (stories)
   (1)

3. What word goes with **when**? different (once)
   (1)

4. What word goes with **just right**? (enough) near
   (1)

5. What word goes with **low**? (high) happy
   (1)

6. What word goes with **sad**? once (happy)
   (1)

7. What word goes with **never**? high (always)
   (1)

8. What word goes with **same**? (different) stories
   (1)

Read directions to children.
High-Frequency Words
153

Assessment Tip: Total 8 points
Grade 1, Unit 6: Three Cheers for Us!

Name _____

Lesson 27
PRACTICE BOOK

What Can You Do?
Phonics: Adding -er, -est
(change y to i)

Adding -*er*, -*est*
(change *y* to *i*)

Read the words. Circle the word that does not belong.

1. fancy fancier fanciest (find)
   (1 point)

2. happy happier (hand) happiest
   (1)

3. silly sillier silliest (still)
   (1)

4. funny (far) funnier funniest
   (1)

5. jolly jollier jolliest (joke)
   (1)

6. messy (miss) messier messiest
   (1)

Read directions to children.
Phonics
154

Assessment Tip: Total 6 points
Grade 1, Unit 6: Three Cheers for Us!

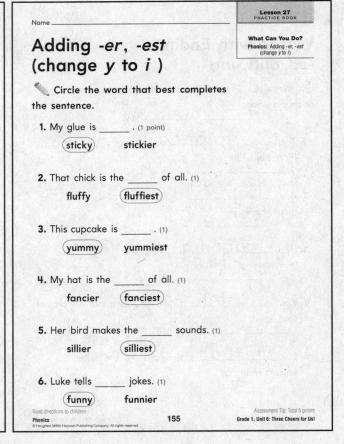

Name _____

Lesson 27
PRACTICE BOOK

What Can You Do?
Phonics: Adding -er, -est
(change y to i)

Adding -*er*, -*est*
(change *y* to *i*)

Circle the word that best completes the sentence.

1. My glue is _____ . (1 point)
   (sticky) stickier

2. That chick is the _____ of all. (1)
   fluffy (fluffiest)

3. This cupcake is _____ . (1)
   (yummy) yummiest

4. My hat is the _____ of all. (1)
   fancier (fanciest)

5. Her bird makes the _____ sounds. (1)
   sillier (silliest)

6. Luke tells _____ jokes. (1)
   (funny) funnier

Read directions to children.
Phonics
155

Assessment Tip: Total 6 points
Grade 1, Unit 6: Three Cheers for Us!

Spelling Words Ending in *-er*, *-est*

🖊 Sort the words. Write the correct Spelling Words in each column.

Spelling Words

hard
harder
hardest
fast
faster
fastest
slow
slower
slowest
sooner

Words with -er	Words with -est
harder (1 point)	hardest (1)
faster (1)	fastest (1)
slower (1)	slowest (1)
sooner (1)	

Base words

hard (1)	fast (1)	slow (1)

Read directions to children.
Spelling
© Houghton Mifflin Harcourt Publishing Company. All rights reserved.
156
Assessment Tip: Total 10 points
Grade 1, Unit 6: Three Cheers For Us!

Question or Exclamation?

🖊 Draw a line from each question to the question mark (?). Draw a line from each exclamation to the exclamation point (!).

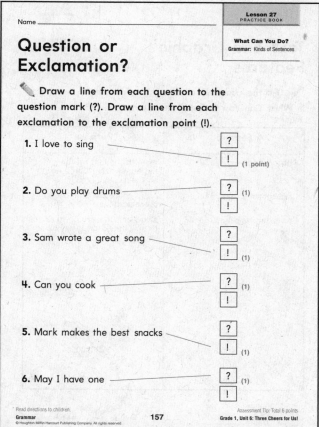

1. I love to sing — [?] [!] (1 point)

2. Do you play drums — [?] (1) [!]

3. Sam wrote a great song — [?] [!] (1)

4. Can you cook — [?] (1) [!]

5. Mark makes the best snacks — [?] [!] (1)

6. May I have one — [?] (1) [!]

Read directions to children.
Grammar
© Houghton Mifflin Harcourt Publishing Company. All rights reserved.
157
Assessment Tip: Total 6 points
Grade 1, Unit 6: Three Cheers for Us!

Write Sentences with *Because*

🖊 Finish these sentences that tell your opinion about learning something new.

Responses will vary.

Topic Sentence

_____

Learning to (1 point) _____ is (1) _____ .

hard   easy

Detail Sentence _____

One reason is (2) _____

_____

Detail Sentence _____

Another reason is (2) _____

_____

Read directions to children.
Writing
© Houghton Mifflin Harcourt Publishing Company. All rights reserved.
158
Assessment Tip: Total 6 points
Grade 1, Unit 6: Three Cheers For Us!

Syllable *-le*

🖊 Circle the word that names the picture.

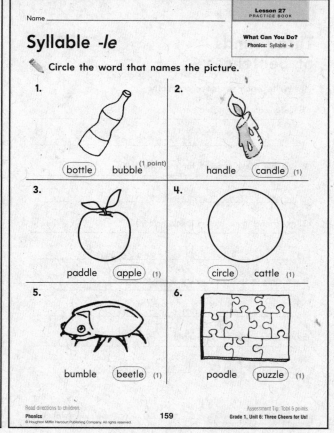

1. (bottle) bubble (1 point)

2. handle (candle) (1)

3. paddle (apple) (1)

4. (circle) cattle (1)

5. bumble (beetle) (1)

6. poodle (puzzle) (1)

Read directions to children.
Phonics
© Houghton Mifflin Harcourt Publishing Company. All rights reserved.
159
Assessment Tip: Total 6 points
Grade 1, Unit 6: Three Cheers for Us!

Text and Graphic Features

✏️ Use the chart to tell about the features
in **What Can You Do?** and their purposes.

Feature	Purpose
Photographs on pp. 56–60	go with the text on the pages; show children doing activities
Photographs on p. 61	show more children doing more activities
Photographs on pp. 63–64 (3 points)	show children trying to do things they aren't very good at (3)

160

Spelling Words Ending in *-er*, *-est*

✏️ Add **-er** to each base word. Then write
the new Spelling Word on the line.

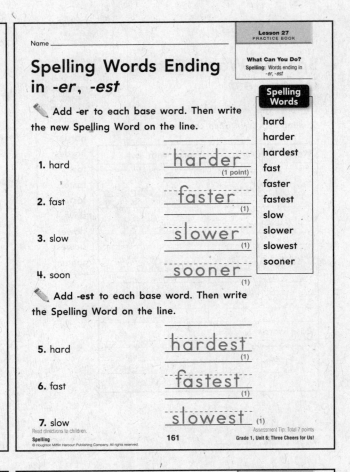

Spelling Words

hard
harder
hardest
fast
faster
fastest
slow
slower
slowest
sooner

1. hard   harder (1 point)

2. fast   faster (1)

3. slow   slower (1)

4. soon   sooner (1)

✏️ Add **-est** to each base word. Then write
the Spelling Word on the line.

5. hard   hardest (1)

6. fast   fastest (1)

7. slow   slowest (1)

161

Three Kinds of Sentences

✏️ Write each sentence correctly.

1. Carly can knit (statement)

    Carly can knit. (2 points)

2. will she make a scarf for me (question)

    Will she make a scarf for me? (2)

3. my friend loves to run (exclamation)

    My friend loves to run! (2)

4. he runs in the park every day (statement)

    He runs in the park every day. (2)

5. what can you do (question)

    What can you do? (2)

162

Planning My Sentences

✏️ Write your opinion. Then write reasons
that tell why. Responses will vary.

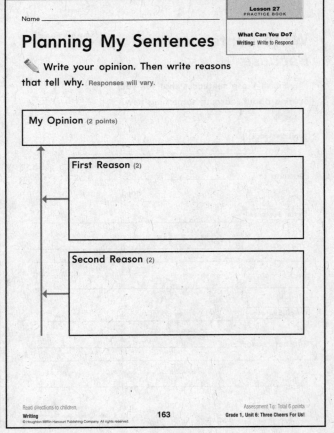

My Opinion (2 points)

First Reason (2)

Second Reason (2)

163

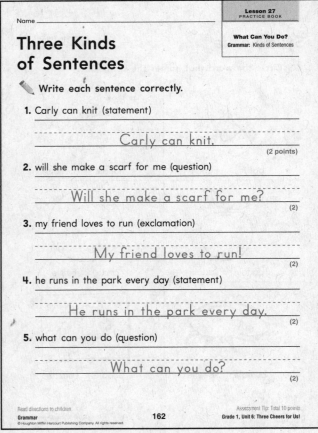

Words with Endings -er and -est

✎ Write the Spelling Word that completes each sentence.

fast	faster	fastest

1. The bus goes __fast__ . (1 point)

2. The truck goes __faster__ than the bus. (1)

3. The car goes the __fastest__ . (1)

slow	slower	slowest

4. The bug is __slow__ . (1)

5. The worm is __slower__ than the bug. (1)

6. The turtle is the __slowest__ of all. (1)

Read directions to children.
Spelling
© Houghton Mifflin Harcourt Publishing Company. All rights reserved.
164
Assessment Tip: Total 6 points
Grade 1, Unit 6: Three Cheers for Us!

Spiral Review

✎ Choose the correct words from the word box to finish each sentence.

Mark	I	me

1. __Mark__ and __I__ act in a play. (2 points)

I	Tammy	Me

2. __Tammy__ and __I__ write stories. (2)

Me	I	Ricky

3. __Ricky__ and __I__ are friends. (2)

I	Me	Sue

4. __Sue__ and __I__ like to slide. (2)

Read directions to children.
Grammar
© Houghton Mifflin Harcourt Publishing Company. All rights reserved.
165
Assessment Tip: Total 8 points
Grade 1, Unit 6: Three Cheers for Us!

Grammar in Writing

A **statement** ends with a period. A **question** ends with a question mark. An **exclamation** ends with an exclamation point. All sentences begin with capital letters.

✎ Revise each sentence. Change it to the kind shown in ( ).

Example: Glen can read. (question)
Can Glen read?

Possible responses shown.

1. Is skating fun? (statement)

__Skating is fun.__ (2 points)

2. I like to ride my bike. (exclamation)

__Riding my bike is my favorite thing to do!__ (2)

3. Chuck likes to act. (question)

__Does Chuck like to act?__ (2)

4. Vicky writes the best stories! (statement)

__Vicky writes stories.__ (2)

Read directions to children.
Grammar
© Houghton Mifflin Harcourt Publishing Company. All rights reserved.
166
Assessment Tip: Total 8 points
Grade 1, Unit 6: Three Cheers for Us!

Words to Know

✎ Circle the correct word in each sentence.

1. The cat plays with a (ball, head) of yarn. (1 point)

2. We all (cried, heard) the crash. (1)

3. You (heard, should) try these grapes. (1)

4. Jean is the (second, ball) girl in line. (1)

5. "Let's go!" (cried, heard) Kenny. (1)

6. My (large, head) hurts. (1)

7. We are running (second, across) the field. (1)

8. There is a (large, heard) bird in the tree. (1)

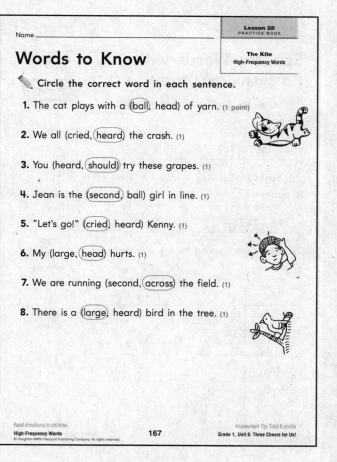

Read directions to children.
High-Frequency Words
© Houghton Mifflin Harcourt Publishing Company. All rights reserved.
167
Assessment Tip: Total 8 points
Grade 1, Unit 6: Three Cheers for Us!

Long *i* Spelling Patterns *igh*, *y*, *ie*

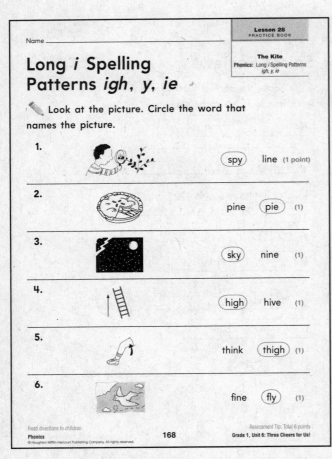

✏️ Look at the picture. Circle the word that names the picture.

Name _____

Lesson 28
PRACTICE BOOK

The Kite
Phonics: Long *i* Spelling Patterns
igh, y, ie

1. (spy) line (1 point)

2. pine (pie) (1)

3. (sky) nine (1)

4. (high) hive (1)

5. think (thigh) (1)

6. fine (fly) (1)

Read directions to children.
Phonics
168
Assessment Tip: Total 6 points
Grade 1, Unit 6: Three Cheers for Us!
© Houghton Mifflin Harcourt Publishing Company. All rights reserved.

Long *i* Spelling Patterns *igh*, *y*, *ie*

Name _____

Lesson 28
PRACTICE BOOK

The Kite
Phonics: Long *i* Spelling Patterns
igh, y, ie

✏️ Write a word from the box to finish each sentence.

thigh	dry	try	tie	high

1. Sam hurt his ___thigh___ (1 point) when he fell.

2. Dad's ___tie___ (1) has dots and stripes.

3. I will ___try___ (1) to swim.

4. The bird will fly up ___high___ (1).

5. The wet shirt will ___dry___ (1).

Read directions to children.
Phonics
169
Assessment Tip: Total 5 points
Grade 1, Unit 6: Three Cheers for Us!
© Houghton Mifflin Harcourt Publishing Company. All rights reserved.

Spelling Words with Patterns *igh*, *y*, *ie*

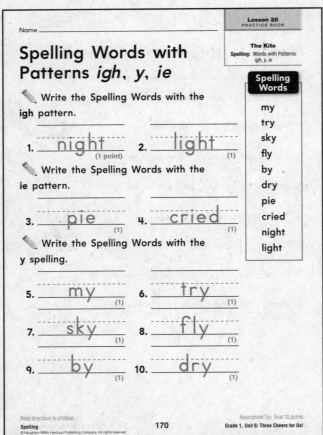

Name _____

Lesson 28
PRACTICE BOOK

The Kite
Spelling: Words with Patterns
igh, y, ie

✏️ Write the Spelling Words with the *igh* pattern.

1. ___night___ (1 point) 2. ___light___ (1)

✏️ Write the Spelling Words with the *ie* pattern.

3. ___pie___ (1) 4. ___cried___ (1)

✏️ Write the Spelling Words with the *y* spelling.

5. ___my___ (1) 6. ___try___ (1)

7. ___sky___ (1) 8. ___fly___ (1)

9. ___by___ (1) 10. ___dry___ (1)

Spelling Words

my
try
sky
fly
by
dry
pie
cried
night
light

Read directions to children.
Spelling
170
Assessment Tip: Total 10 points
Grade 1, Unit 6: Three Cheers for Us!
© Houghton Mifflin Harcourt Publishing Company. All rights reserved.

Adjectives for Taste and Smell

✏️ Draw a line under each adjective. Then write the adjective.

1. I smell the sweet roses.

___sweet___ (2 points)

2. We taste the bitter lemon.

___bitter___ (2)

3. Does the milk smell sour?

___sour___ (2)

4. The chips taste spicy.

___spicy___ (2)

5. The toast smells burnt.

___burnt___ (2)

Read directions to children.
Grammar
171
Assessment Tip: Total 10 points
Grade 1, Unit 6: Three Cheers for Us!
© Houghton Mifflin Harcourt Publishing Company. All rights reserved.

Using Different Words

The Kite
Writing: Write to Respond

Change a repeated word to an exact word. Use a word from the box or your own.

bright	down	high
flew	funny	blue
mean	ran	sunny

Sample answers.

Toad <u>went</u> fast, and the kite <u>went</u> up.

Toad ___ran___ (2 points) fast, and the kite went up.

The <u>little</u> birds laughed at Toad's <u>little</u> kite.

The little birds laughed at Toad's ___funny___ (2) kite.

The <u>pretty</u> kite danced in the <u>pretty</u> sky.

The pretty kite danced in the ___bright___ (2) sky.

Read directions to children.
Writing
© Houghton Mifflin Harcourt Publishing Company. All rights reserved.
172
Assessment Tip: Total 6 points
Grade 1, Unit 6: Three Cheers For Us!

Adding -ed, -ing, -er, -est, -es

The Kite
Phonics: Adding -ed, -ing, -er, -est, -es

Write the word that best completes each sentence. Use words from the box.

smaller	jumped	riding	highest	foxes

1. Those trees are the ___highest___ (1 point) of all.

2. That bird is ___smaller___ (1) than this one.

3. Who is ___riding___ (1) a red bike?

4. A frog ___jumped___ (1) into the pond.

5. Five ___foxes___ (1) ran to the woods.

Read directions to children.
Phonics
© Houghton Mifflin Harcourt Publishing Company. All rights reserved.
173
Assessment Tip: Total 5 points
Grade 1, Unit 6: Three Cheers for Us!

Story Structure

The Kite
Comprehension: Story Structure

Use the Story Map to tell about the characters, setting, and plot of **The Kite**.

Characters	Setting
Frog, Toad, and three robins (2 points)	on a windy day in a meadow (2)

Plot

Beginning

Frog and Toad go to a meadow to fly a kite.

They can't get the kite to fly.

Middle

First, Toad runs with the kite.

Then, he runs and waves the kite over his head.

Next, he runs, waves the kite over his head, and jumps up and down.

End

Finally, he runs, waves the kite over his head, jumps up and down, and shouts, "UP, KITE, UP!"

The kite flies, and Frog and Toad sit and watch it. (6)

Read directions to children.
Comprehension
© Houghton Mifflin Harcourt Publishing Company. All rights reserved.
174
Assessment Tip: Total 10 points
Grade 1, Unit 6: Three Cheers for Us!

Spelling Words with Patterns igh, y, ie

The Kite
Spelling: Words with Patterns igh, y, ie

Spelling Words
my
try
sky
fly
by
dry
pie
cried
night
light

Write each group of Spelling Words in ABC order.

my	try	dry	pie
sky	fly	cried	night
by		light	

by (1 point)	cried (1)
fly (1)	dry (1)
my (1)	light (1)
sky (1)	night (1)
try (1)	pie (1)

Read directions to children.
Spelling
© Houghton Mifflin Harcourt Publishing Company. All rights reserved.
175
Assessment Tip: Total 10 points
Grade 1, Unit 6: Three Cheers For Us!

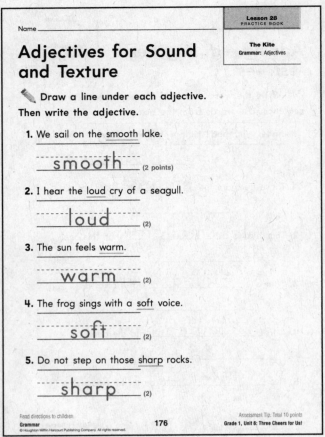

Adjectives for Sound and Texture

✏️ Draw a line under each adjective. Then write the adjective.

1. We sail on the smooth lake.

   smooth (2 points)

2. I hear the loud cry of a seagull.

   loud (2)

3. The sun feels warm.

   warm (2)

4. The frog sings with a soft voice.

   soft (2)

5. Do not step on those sharp rocks.

   sharp (2)

176

Assessment Tip: Total 10 points
Grade 1, Unit 6: Three Cheers for Us!

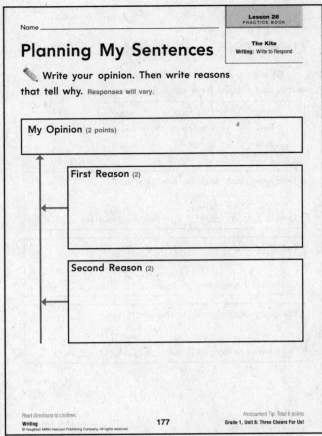

Planning My Sentences

✏️ Write your opinion. Then write reasons that tell why. Responses will vary.

My Opinion (2 points)

First Reason (2)

Second Reason (2)

177

Assessment Tip: Total 6 points
Grade 1, Unit 6: Three Cheers For Us!

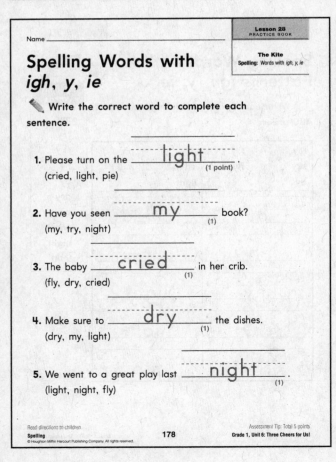

Spelling Words with *igh, y, ie*

✏️ Write the correct word to complete each sentence.

1. Please turn on the ___ light ___ .
   (cried, light, pie) (1 point)

2. Have you seen ___ my ___ book?
   (my, try, night) (1)

3. The baby ___ cried ___ in her crib.
   (fly, dry, cried) (1)

4. Make sure to ___ dry ___ the dishes.
   (dry, my, light) (1)

5. We went to a great play last ___ night ___ .
   (light, night, fly) (1)

178

Assessment Tip: Total 5 points
Grade 1, Unit 6: Three Cheers for Us!

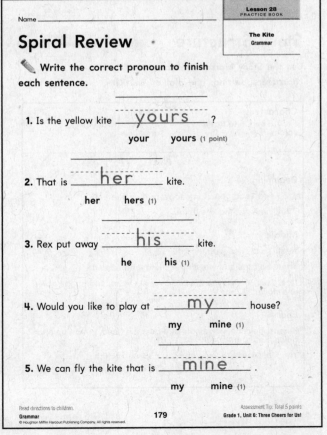

Spiral Review

✏️ Write the correct pronoun to finish each sentence.

1. Is the yellow kite ___ yours ___ ?
   your   yours (1 point)

2. That is ___ her ___ kite.
   her   hers (1)

3. Rex put away ___ his ___ kite.
   he   his (1)

4. Would you like to play at ___ my ___ house?
   my   mine (1)

5. We can fly the kite that is ___ mine ___ .
   my   mine (1)

179

Assessment Tip: Total 5 points
Grade 1, Unit 6: Three Cheers for Us!

Grammar in Writing

Some adjectives describe nouns by telling about **taste**, **smell**, **sound**, or **feel**.

Example: I feel the breeze.
(cool, ^)

✏️ Revise each sentence. Use the proofreading mark to add an adjective.

| sweet | fresh | happy | soft |

Possible responses shown.

1. Mr. Bee shares some honey. (2 points)
(sweet)

2. The frog gave a croak. (2)
(happy)

3. We sit on the grass. (2)
(soft)

4. We enjoy the air. (2)
(fresh)

Proofreading Mark	
∧	add

180

Words to Know

✏️ Circle the correct word to complete each sentence.

1. Raking the yard is a good (any, **idea**). (1 point)

2. The (**leaves**, happened) are a pretty red. (1)

3. Summer is (**gone**, any), and fall is here. (1)

4. Bill is (**behind**, almost) the tree. (1)

5. Sal waves (**hello**, gone) to Bess. (1)

6. What (behind, **happened**) when Bill jumped in the leaves? (1)

7. (Idea, **Any**) pal can help us rake. (1)

8. We are (leaves, **almost**) done raking. (1)

181

Suffixes *-ful*, *-ly*, *-y*

✏️ Write a suffix from the box to finish the word.

| ful | ly | y |

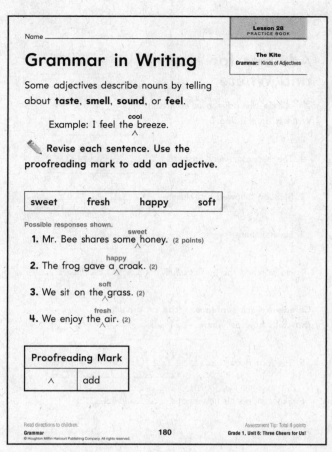

1. sad **ly** (1 point)

2. bump **y** (1)

3. dust **y** (1)

4. help **ful** (1)

5. slow **ly** (1)

6. safe **ly** (1)

182

Suffixes *-ful*, *-ly*, *-y*

✏️ Choose a word from the box. Choose a suffix to make a new word. Write the new word below the suffix.

| spoon | snow | sad | trick |
| joy | quick | peace | dirt | glad |

y	ly	ful
snowy (1 point)	sadly (1)	spoonful (1)
tricky (1)	gladly (1)	joyful (1)
dirty (1)	quickly (1)	peaceful (1)

183

Spelling Words with the Suffixes -ly, -y, -ful

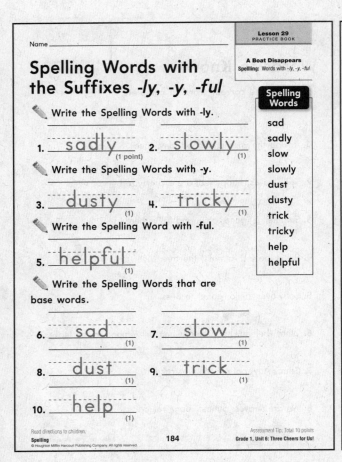

✎ Write the Spelling Words with -ly.

1. __sadly__ (1 point)   2. __slowly__ (1)

✎ Write the Spelling Words with -y.

3. __dusty__ (1)   4. __tricky__ (1)

✎ Write the Spelling Word with -ful.

5. __helpful__ (1)

✎ Write the Spelling Words that are base words.

6. __sad__ (1)   7. __slow__ (1)

8. __dust__ (1)   9. __trick__ (1)

10. __help__ (1)

Spelling Words

sad
sadly
slow
slowly
dust
dusty
trick
tricky
help
helpful

Read directions to children.
Spelling
© Houghton Mifflin Harcourt Publishing Company. All rights reserved.
184
Assessment Tip: Total 10 points
Grade 1, Unit 6: Three Cheers for Us!

Adverbs for How and Where

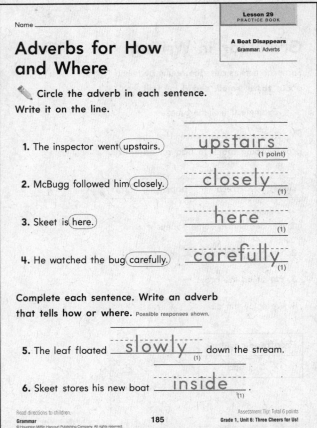

✎ Circle the adverb in each sentence. Write it on the line.

1. The inspector went (upstairs.)   __upstairs__ (1 point)

2. McBugg followed him (closely.)   __closely__ (1)

3. Skeet is (here.)   __here__ (1)

4. He watched the bug (carefully.)   __carefully__ (1)

Complete each sentence. Write an adverb that tells **how** or **where**. Possible responses shown.

5. The leaf floated __slowly__ (1) down the stream.

6. Skeet stores his new boat __inside__ (1).

Read directions to children.
Grammar
© Houghton Mifflin Harcourt Publishing Company. All rights reserved.
185
Assessment Tip: Total 6 points
Grade 1, Unit 6: Three Cheers for Us!

Giving Examples

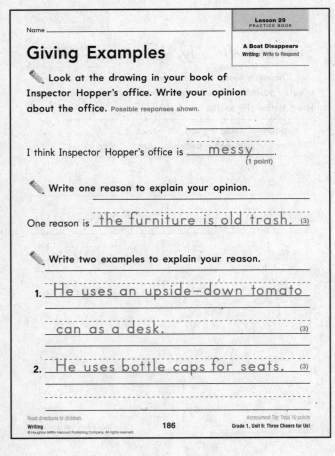

✎ Look at the drawing in your book of Inspector Hopper's office. Write your opinion about the office. Possible responses shown.

I think Inspector Hopper's office is __messy__ (1 point).

✎ Write one reason to explain your opinion.

One reason is __the furniture is old trash.__ (3)

✎ Write two examples to explain your reason.

1. __He uses an upside-down tomato can as a desk.__ (3)

2. __He uses bottle caps for seats.__ (3)

Read directions to children.
Writing
© Houghton Mifflin Harcourt Publishing Company. All rights reserved.
186
Assessment Tip: Total 10 points
Grade 1, Unit 6: Three Cheers for Us!

Long Vowel Spelling Patterns a, e, i, o, u

✎ Circle the two words in each row that rhyme. Then write the letter that spells the long vowel sound.

1. (table) hi (fable) me   __a__ (1 point)

2. hi (she) (he) go   __e__ (1)

3. (kind) no flu (mind)   __i__ (1)

4. (flu) (Stu) so be   __u__ (1)

5. we (hold) wind (told)   __o__ (1)

Read directions to children.
Phonics
© Houghton Mifflin Harcourt Publishing Company. All rights reserved.
187
Assessment Tip: Total 5 points
Grade 1, Unit 6: Three Cheers for Us!

Cause and Effect

✎ Use the chart to write about what happened in **A Boat Disappears** and why it happened.

What Happened?	Why Did It Happen?
Skeet walks into Inspector Hopper's office.	He wants to tell the inspector his boat disappeared.
Inspector Hopper says he will take Skeet's case.	He wants to find Skeet's boat.
They go to the lake.	The lake is the last place where Skeet saw his boat.
They follow a trail of pieces of Skeet's boat. (4 points)	They hope the trail will lead them to Skeet's boat. (4)

Read directions to children.
Comprehension
© Houghton Mifflin Harcourt Publishing Company. All rights reserved.
188
Assessment Tip: Total 8 points
Grade 1, Unit 6: Three Cheers for Us!

Spelling Words with the Suffixes -ly, -y, -ful

Spelling Words
- sad
- sadly
- slow
- slowly
- dust
- dusty
- trick
- tricky
- help
- helpful

✎ Add -ly to each base word. Then write the new Spelling Word on the line.

1. sad   sadly (1 point)

2. slow   slowly (1)

✎ Add -y to each base word. Then write the new Spelling Word on the line.

3. dust   dusty (1)

4. trick   tricky (1)

✎ Add -ful to the base word. Then write the new Spelling Word on the line.

5. help   helpful (1)

Read directions to children.
Spelling
© Houghton Mifflin Harcourt Publishing Company. All rights reserved.
189
Assessment Tip: Total 5 points
Grade 1, Unit 6: Three Cheers for Us!

Adverbs for When and How Much

✎ Circle the adverb in each sentence. Write it on the line.

1. The water is (too) high to cross.   too (1 point)

2. Skeet arrived (late) to the picnic.   late (1)

3. He was (very) happy to see his friends.   very (1)

4. They will have a boat race (soon.)   soon (1)

✎ Complete each sentence. Write an adverb that tells when or how much. Possible responses shown.

5. We will have a picnic _____ tomorrow _____ (1)

6. The bucket was _____ totally _____ full. (1)

Read directions to children.
Grammar
© Houghton Mifflin Harcourt Publishing Company. All rights reserved.
190
Assessment Tip: Total 6 points
Grade 1, Unit 6: Three Cheers for Us!

Words with the Suffixes -ly, -y, -ful

✎ Write the correct word from the box to complete each sentence.

1. I did a card _____ trick _____ (1 point)   [trick / tricky]

2. It was _____ tricky _____ to find the way to the park. (1)   [trick / tricky]

3. I like to _____ help _____ wash the car. (1)   [help / helpful]

4. When I wash the car, I am very _____ helpful _____ (1)   [help / helpful]

5. I was _____ sad _____ to hear my mom call me home. (1)   [sad / sadly]

6. I _____ sadly _____ (1) walked home.   [sad / sadly]

Read directions to children.
Spelling
© Houghton Mifflin Harcourt Publishing Company. All rights reserved.
191
Assessment Tip: Total 6 points
Grade 1, Unit 6: Three Cheers for Us!

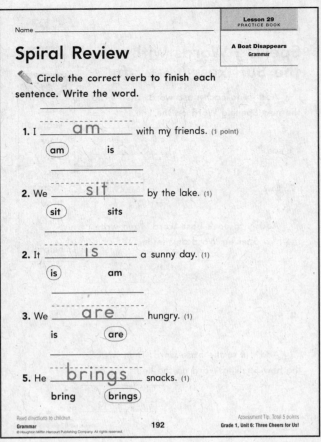

Spiral Review

🖊 Circle the correct verb to finish each
sentence. Write the word.

1. I _____ am _____ with my friends. (1 point)

   (am)   is

2. We _____ sit _____ by the lake. (1)

   (sit)   sits

2. It _____ is _____ a sunny day. (1)

   (is)   am

3. We _____ are _____ hungry. (1)

   is   (are)

5. He _____ brings _____ snacks. (1)

   bring   (brings)

Read directions to children.
Grammar
© Houghton Mifflin Harcourt Publishing Company. All rights reserved.
192
Assessment Tip: Total 5 points
Grade 1, Unit 6: Three Cheers for Us!

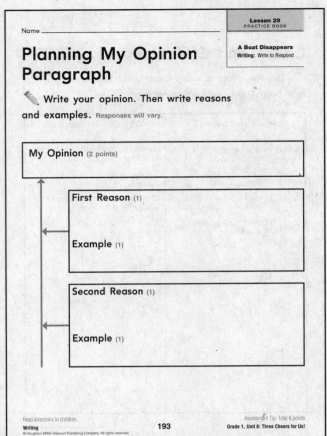

Planning My Opinion Paragraph

🖊 Write your opinion. Then write reasons
and examples. Responses will vary.

My Opinion (2 points)

First Reason (1)

Example (1)

Second Reason (1)

Example (1)

Read directions to children.
Writing
© Houghton Mifflin Harcourt Publishing Company. All rights reserved.
193
Assessment Tip: Total 6 points
Grade 1, Unit 6: Three Cheers for Us!

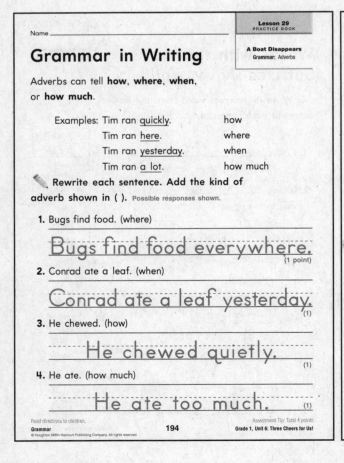

Grammar in Writing

Adverbs can tell **how**, **where**, **when**,
or **how much**.

Examples: Tim ran quickly.   how
           Tim ran here.   where
           Tim ran yesterday.   when
           Tim ran a lot.   how much

🖊 **Rewrite each sentence. Add the kind of
adverb shown in ( ).** Possible responses shown.

1. Bugs find food. (where)

   Bugs find food everywhere.
                              (1 point)

2. Conrad ate a leaf. (when)

   Conrad ate a leaf yesterday.
                              (1)

3. He chewed. (how)

   He chewed quietly.
                              (1)

4. He ate. (how much)

   He ate too much.
                              (1)

Read directions to children.
Grammar
© Houghton Mifflin Harcourt Publishing Company. All rights reserved.
194
Assessment Tip: Total 4 points
Grade 1, Unit 6: Three Cheers for Us!

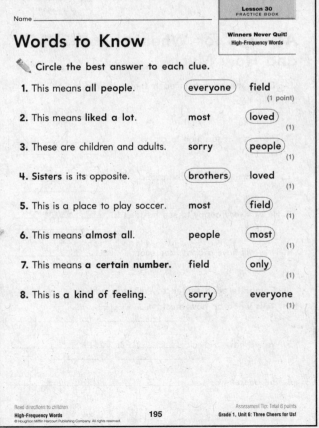

Words to Know

🖊 Circle the best answer to each clue.

1. This means all people.   (everyone)   field
                                                 (1 point)
2. This means liked a lot.   most   (loved)
                                                   (1)
3. These are children and adults.   sorry   (people)
                                                   (1)
4. Sisters is its opposite.   (brothers)   loved
                                                   (1)
5. This is a place to play soccer. most   (field)
                                                   (1)
6. This means almost all.   people   (most)
                                                   (1)
7. This means a certain number.   field   (only)
                                                   (1)
8. This is a kind of feeling.   (sorry)   everyone
                                                   (1)

Read directions to children.
High-Frequency Words
© Houghton Mifflin Harcourt Publishing Company. All rights reserved.
195
Assessment Tip: Total 8 points
Grade 1, Unit 6: Three Cheers for Us!

Syllable Pattern CV

✏️ Read each word. Draw a line to divide the CV word into two syllables.

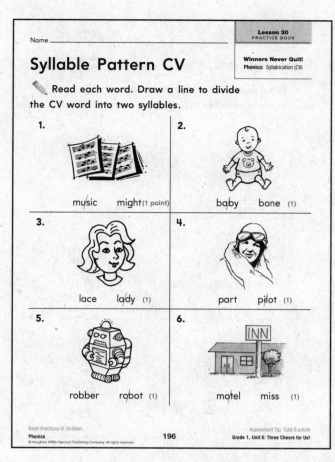

1. mu|sic   might (1 point)

2. ba|by   bone (1)

3. lace   la|dy (1)

4. part   pi|lot (1)

5. robber   ro|bot (1)

6. mo|tel   miss (1)

Read directions to children.
Phonics
© Houghton Mifflin Harcourt Publishing Company. All rights reserved.
196
Assessment Tip: Total 6 points
Grade 1, Unit 6: Three Cheers for Us!

Syllable Pattern CV

✏️ In each sentence, circle the CV word that has two syllables.

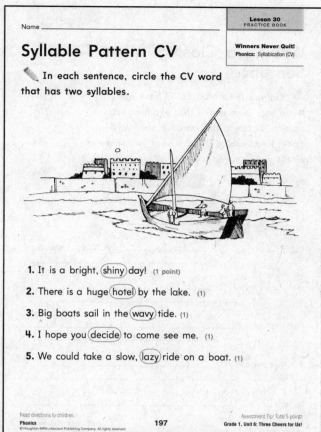

1. It is a bright, (shiny) day! (1 point)

2. There is a huge (hotel) by the lake. (1)

3. Big boats sail in the (wavy) tide. (1)

4. I hope you (decide) to come see me. (1)

5. We could take a slow, (lazy) ride on a boat. (1)

Read directions to children.
Phonics
© Houghton Mifflin Harcourt Publishing Company. All rights reserved.
197
Assessment Tip: Total 5 points
Grade 1, Unit 6: Three Cheers for Us!

Spelling Words with CV Syllables

Spelling Words
even
open
begin
baby
tiger
music
paper
zero
table
below

✏️ Write the Spelling Words with the long e sound in the first syllable.

1. even (1 point)   2. begin (1)

3. zero (1)   4. below (1)

✏️ Write the Spelling Words with the long a sound in the first syllable.

5. baby (1)   6. paper (1)

7. table (1)

✏️ Write the Spelling Words with these long vowel sounds in the first syllable.

8. long i tiger (1)   9. long o open (1)

10. long u music (1)

Read directions to children.
Spelling
© Houghton Mifflin Harcourt Publishing Company. All rights reserved.
198
Assessment Tip: Total 10 points
Grade 1, Unit 6: Three Cheers for Us!

Adjectives with *er* and *est*

✏️ Circle the correct adjective to finish each sentence. Write the adjective.

1. Tim is ___taller___ than Max.
(taller)   tallest (1 point)

2. Fred is the ___tallest___ of them all.
taller   (tallest) (1)

3. Cathy is ___older___ than Cam.
(older)   oldest (1)

4. Adam is the ___smallest___ player of all.
smaller   (smallest) (1)

Read directions to children.
Grammar
© Houghton Mifflin Harcourt Publishing Company. All rights reserved.
199
Assessment Tip: Total 4 points
Grade 1, Unit 6: Three Cheers for Us!

Writing a Closing Sentence

✎ Do you think Mia should have quit?
Write your own words that explain your
opinion. Listen to the words in the Word
Bank. Read along. Be sure your last sentence
retells your opinion. Responses will vary.

Word Bank

agree   disagree   decision   reason   example

_____

I (1 point) _____ with Mia's decision to

_____

quit. One reason is (1) _____

_____

For example, (1) _____ .

_____

Another reason is (1) _____

_____

I think (1) _____

Read directions and Word Bank to children.
Writing
© Houghton Mifflin Harcourt Publishing Company. All rights reserved.
200
Assessment Tip: Total 5 points
Grade 1, Unit 6: Three Cheers for Us!

Name _____

Lesson 30
PRACTICE BOOK

Winners Never Quit!
Phonics: Words with Prefixes
un-, re-

Prefixes un-, re-

✎ Read each word. Circle the word in
each box that matches the picture.

1.	2.
(untie) tried (1 point)	read (repaint) (1)
3.	4.
setting (remove) (1)	bedding (unbraid) (1)
5.	6.
(untidy) neat (1)	unzip (unbutton) (1)

Read directions to children.
Phonics
© Houghton Mifflin Harcourt Publishing Company. All rights reserved.
201
Assessment Tip: Total 6 points
Grade 1, Unit 6: Three Cheers for Us!

Name _____

Lesson 30
PRACTICE BOOK

Winners Never Quit!
Comprehension: Understanding
Characters

Understanding Characters

✎ Use the chart to tell what Mia thinks, what
she says, and what she does in **Winners Never
Quit!**

Thinks	Says	Does
Mia doesn't like to lose.	"I quit!" (1 point)	Mia plays soccer.
Mia would rather quit than lose.		One day, Mia can't score a goal.
Mia finds out that playing is more important than winning or losing. (3)		Mia has to stand by the side and watch her brothers and sisters play soccer without her.
		Mia doesn't score a goal.
		She keeps playing and tries again. (4)

Read directions to children.
Comprehension
© Houghton Mifflin Harcourt Publishing Company. All rights reserved.
202
Assessment Tip: Total 8 points
Grade 1, Unit 6: Three Cheers for Us!

Name _____

Lesson 30
PRACTICE BOOK

Winners Never Quit!
Spelling: Words with
Syllables CV

Spelling Words with Syllables CV

✎ Write the Spelling Word that fits
each clue.

Spelling Words

even
open
begin
baby
tiger
music
paper
zero
table
below

1. Opposite of **closed**   open (1 point)

2. A very young person   baby (1)

3. Something to listen to   music (1)

4. Opposite of **end**   begin (1)

5. Opposite of **above**   below (1)

6. An animal   tiger (1)

Read directions to children.
Spelling
© Houghton Mifflin Harcourt Publishing Company. All rights reserved.
203
Assessment Tip: Total 6 points
Grade 1, Unit 6: Three Cheers for Us!

Name _____

Using the Right Adjective

Write adjectives from the Word Banks to finish the sentences.

Word Bank

green   greener   greenest

1. Our yard is __green__ . (1 point)

2. Your yard is __greener__ than ours. (1)

3. His yard is the __greenest__ of all. (1)

Word Bank

long   longer   longest

4. We played a __long__ game today. (1)

5. The game yesterday was __longer__ than the game today. (1)

Assessment Tip: Total 5 points
Grade 1, Unit 6: Three Cheers for Us!

Name _____

Lesson 30
PRACTICE BOOK

Winners Never Quit!
Spelling: Words with Syllable Pattern CV

Spelling Words with Syllable Pattern CV

Write the correct word to complete each sentence.

1. Ken saw a __tiger__ at the zoo. (1 point)
(below, tiger)

2. Please sit and __begin__ your test. (1)
(even, begin)

3. What kind of __music__ do you like? (1)
(below, music)

4. I used red __paper__ to make the card. (1)
(paper, zero)

5. The food is on the __table__ . (1)
(open, table)

Assessment Tip: Total 5 points
Grade 1, Unit 6: Three Cheers for Us!

Name _____

Spiral Review

Choose contractions from the box for the underlined words. Write the contractions.

1. She is a tennis player.

__She's__ (2 points)

2. I cannot wait to play with her.

__can't__ (2)

3. It is not hard to play.

__isn't__ (2)

4. He is learning now!

__He's__ (2)

Word Bank

He's
can't
She's
isn't

Assessment Tip: Total 8 points
Grade 1, Unit 6: Three Cheers for Us!

Name _____

Grammar in Writing

- Add **er** to adjectives to compare two.
- Add **est** to compare more than two.

   Example: Today is warm.
   Today is the warmest day of the summer.

Revise each sentence. Use an adjective that compares. Add other words, too.

Possible responses shown.

1. Beth is a fast runner.

__Beth is the fastest runner on her team.__
(2 points)

2. Tad is tall.

__Tad is taller than Mike.__ (2)

3. Our team is stronger.

__Our team is the strongest in town.__ (2)

4. Today was cold.

__Today was colder than yesterday.__ (2)

Assessment Tip: Total 8 points
Grade 1, Unit 6: Three Cheers for Us!
